FLORIDA
SCHOOL SHOOTING

BY MARCIA AMIDON LUSTED

CONTENT CONSULTANT
JULIE A. WEBBER, PROFESSOR
DEPARTMENT OF POLITICS AND GOVERNMENT
ILLINOIS STATE UNIVERSITY

Essential Library

An Imprint of Abdo Publishing | abdopublishing.com

abdopublishing.com

Published by Abdo Publishing, a division of ABDO, PO Box 398166, Minneapolis,
Minnesota 55439. Copyright © 2019 by Abdo Consulting Group, Inc. International
copyrights reserved in all countries. No part of this book may be reproduced in
any form without written permission from the publisher. Essential Library™ is a
trademark and logo of Abdo Publishing.

Printed in the United States of America, North Mankato, Minnesota
072018
092018

Cover Photo: Joe Raedle/Getty Images News/Getty Images
Interior Photos: Amy Beth Bennett/South Florida Sun-Sentinel/AP Images, 4–5,
18–19, 31, 35; Mike Stocker/South Florida Sun-Sentinel/AP Images, 11; John McCall/
South Florida Sun-Sentinel/AP Images, 14; Abaca Press/Sipa USA/AP Images, 17;
Taimy Alvarez/South Florida Sun-Sentinel/AP Images, 23; Timothy A. Clary/AFP/
Getty Images, 28–29; Wilfredo Lee/AP Images, 37; Mary Altaffer/AP Images, 38–39;
Joe Raedle/Getty Images News/Getty Images, 40–41; Matt McClain/The Washington
Post/Getty Images, 46; Emilee McGovern/SOPA Images/LightRocket/Getty Images,
48–49, 67; Steven Senne/AP Images, 54; Mark Wallheiser/AP Images, 58, 94;
Alex Brandon/AP Images, 60–61, 75; Andrew Harnik/AP Images, 65; Jacquelyn
Martin/AP Images, 70; Scott Serio/ESW/Cal Sport Media/AP Images, 76–77; Olivier
Douliery/picture-alliance/dpa/AP Images, 78; Sue Ogrocki/AP Images, 85; Olivier
Douliery/Abaca Press/Sipa USA/AP Images, 88–89; Michael Laughlin/South Florida
Sun-Sentinel/AP Images, 99

Editor: Alyssa Krekelberg
Series Designer: Maggie Villaume

Library of Congress Control Number: 2018938207

Cataloging-in-Publication Data

Names: Lusted, Marcia Amidon, author.
Title: Florida school shooting / by Marcia Amidon Lusted.
Description: Minneapolis, Minnesota : Abdo Publishing, 2019. | Series: Special
        Reports | Includes online resources and index.
Identifiers: ISBN 9781532116100 (lib.bdg.) | ISBN 9781532157097 (ebook)
Subjects: LCSH: School shootings--Juvenile literature. | School violence--
        Juvenile literature. | Schools--Safety measures--Juvenile literature. |
        Florida--Juvenile literature.
Classification: DDC 371.782--dc23

CONTENTS

CHAPTER ONE

FEBRUARY 14, 2018

I t was a regular Wednesday afternoon at Marjory Stoneman Douglas (MSD) High School in Parkland, Florida. Students were in class at 2:19 p.m. when an Uber ride-sharing car pulled up outside the school. Nikolas Cruz, a 19-year-old former student of the high school, got out of the back seat. He was carrying a black duffel bag and a backpack. Because it was toward the end of the school day, the school's gates were open and he was able to enter the school campus easily.

"YOU'D BETTER GET OUT OF HERE"

In the months following the shooting, officials developed a rough timeline of what they believed happened. Cruz entered Building 12 of the high school.

Parents prayed and consoled each other as they waited to hear news about their loved ones.

This three-story structure contained some classrooms. Cruz entered the east stairwell of the building just two minutes after he arrived on the campus. He climbed to the second floor, took an AR-15 rifle out of his duffle bag, and began loading it. A freshman named Chris McKenna saw Cruz in the hallway. "You'd better get out of here," Cruz told him. "Things are gonna start getting messy."[1] McKenna immediately ran away.

Cruz began shooting. As soon as he did, the school went into a procedure called Code Red. This locked the fire doors in the hallways and required students and staff to take shelter inside their classrooms. But then the fire alarm went off. Cruz had pulled it because he knew that the alarm would override the Code Red and force students into the halls. Many students later said they were confused by the alarm because they'd just had a fire drill earlier in the day. Cruz wore a gas mask and had smoke grenades.

Meanwhile, McKenna found assistant football coach Aaron Feis and told him about what he'd just seen. Feis said, "Let me go check it out."[2] He left McKenna at the school's baseball field and returned to Building 12. As Cruz was shooting, Feis ran down the hallway. He pushed

MORE TO THE
STORY

THE AR-15

Since the mid-2000s, the AR-15 has been used in several deadly mass shootings. But what exactly is this gun? *AR-15* has become a term used for a range of semiautomatic rifles that are made by several different manufacturers. *AR* does not mean *automatic rifle*. The name comes from the original manufacturer of the gun, ArmaLite, although ArmaLite later sold the patent to Colt's Manufacturing Company. Colt's, which has been in business since the 1850s, also produces pistols, revolvers, rifles, ammunition, and accessories for firearms.

The gun was developed in the 1950s as a military weapon and became standard issue for US soldiers in the Vietnam War (1954–1975). The military version was known as the M-16. When Colt's patents for the AR-15 expired in the 1970s, many other gun manufacturers began making their own versions of the AR-15. *AR-15* became the overall generic name for these rifles. AR-15s are very popular with gun owners, with an estimated eight million in circulation in the United States.[3] They are semiautomatic, which means that the shooter must pull the trigger for each shot. This is different from an automatic rifle, where a shooter can pull and hold the trigger and the weapon will keep firing until it runs out of ammunition. Ownership of automatic weapons is subject to extremely tight restrictions in the United States.

nearby students to safety, using his own body to shield a freshman girl from the bullets. Feis was then shot and killed.

STUDENTS HIDE

In classroom 1232, teacher Shanthi Viswanathan heard shooting. She told her Algebra II students to get on the floor in the corner, and she placed paper over the classroom's interior window so that no one could see in from the hallway. In Room 1214, bullets traveled through the door's glass window and hit six students in a history class, killing two of them.[4]

In classroom 1216, everyone flattened themselves on the floor as soon as they heard the shots, and bullets flew into the room. English teacher Dara Hass said:

> I called 911 and texted to my husband that my students have been shot and to call 911. I hugged the students who did their best to hide under and behind my desk. I communicated

"I WAS HIDING IN A CLOSET FOR 2 HOURS. IT WAS ABOUT GUNS. YOU WEREN'T THERE, YOU DON'T KNOW HOW IT FELT. GUNS GIVE THESE DISGUSTING PEOPLE THE ABILITY TO KILL OTHER HUMAN BEINGS."[5]

—CARLY NOVELL, A STUDENT AT MSD HIGH SCHOOL

nonverbally to the students hiding across the room. These
students witnessed three of their classmates and friends pass. We
sat in silence while the 911 operator told us she was with us and
help was on the way. I held back tears and panic as I hugged my
students.[6]

Geography teacher Scott Beigel was shot after he unlocked a door to his classroom so that students could get in and hide. A student, Peter Wang, held open an outside door to help students in a hallway get out of the building. He too was shot and killed. On a video of the shooting, which later circulated widely on social media, one student was yelling, "Oh my God! Oh my God!" over and over as more than 40 gunshots could be heard in the background.[7]

Moises Lobaton, a senior, was in a psychology class when the shooting started. The students in the class tried to get as far away from the door as possible and hide behind the teacher's desk, but there wasn't enough room for everyone to fit. Shots broke through the window, and a boy was shot in

"THE SHOTS WERE SOMETHING I'LL NEVER FORGET. IT SOUNDED LIKE BOMBS GOING OFF, ONE AT A TIME. IF I WAS ONE OR TWO FEET TO THE RIGHT, I WOULD HAVE DIED."[8]

—MOISES LOBATON, A STUDENT AT MSD HIGH SCHOOL

the arm and began bleeding heavily. His classmates wrapped his arm in cloth to help stop the bleeding, while another boy called 911. Seventeen people died as a result of the shooting.[9]

RESPONDING TO THE THREAT

Most parents got the first news of the situation at the high school when they began receiving text messages from their children inside the school. Noah Krooks, a freshman at the school, texted his father, Howard, at 2:38 p.m. Krooks said he believed there was a shooter in the school, and his father immediately asked if he was safe. Other parents received texts from their children. Some

Police evacuated students from MSD High School as quickly as they could.

students told their parents to text, not call, so their phones wouldn't make any noise and alert the shooter.

As soon as the police arrived, students began exiting the school. Some walked in long lines with hands on the shoulders of the students in front of them. Others held their hands in the air. Some just fled, running as fast as possible. As they came out, heavily armed law enforcement officials swarmed into the buildings. They did not know that Cruz was among the fleeing students. He had discarded his rifle, a bulletproof vest, and his ammunition in a stairwell, so he blended in easily. He exited Building 12 with the other students.

Cruz walked to a nearby Walmart and bought a drink at the Subway restaurant inside. He also stopped at a McDonald's restaurant. He was walking down a residential street in the nearby town of Coral Springs at 3:41 p.m. when police stopped him. The arresting officer, Michael Leonard, said, "He looked like a typical high school student, and for a quick moment I thought, could this be the person who I need to stop?"[11] Cruz was arrested without incident.

WHERE WAS THE ARMED OFFICER?

MSD High School had an armed school resource officer. A resource officer is a law enforcement officer employed in a school to provide security and to prevent crime and juvenile delinquency. These officers are supposed to provide a safe educational environment. Officer Scot Peterson was on the campus at the time of the shootings, armed and in uniform. However, video footage from the school's security cameras showed that Peterson took a position on the west side of Building 12 when the shooting started and never entered the building itself. He did use his radio and positioned himself so that he could see the west entrance of the building. But according to the Broward County sheriff, Peterson should have entered the building and confronted and, if necessary, killed the shooter.

Peterson later said he took actions that he believed were appropriate based on what he knew about the situation. He thought the shots were coming from outside and he took up a tactical position there in response. As the first member of the sheriff's department to report the shots, he also provided SWAT team members with keys to the building, drew maps of the campus and the buildings, and helped school personnel with security video footage.

Police who reported to the scene were hampered by the fact that the school's video surveillance was on a 20-minute time delay. It caused confusion because the police did not know this, and they thought they were seeing Cruz's movements in real time. When they thought he was on the second floor, he had already moved to another area.

WAITING

For parents whose children were inside the high school, waiting for news was agonizing. Some arrived at a nearby

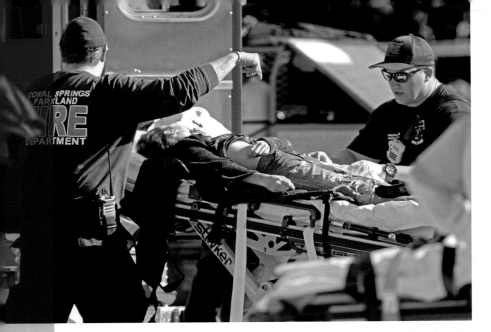

First responders rushed to help victims of the shooting.

hotel, as they were told not to come to the school, and they waited to be reunited with their children. Others stood on the sidewalk outside the school's campus, pacing and calling their children's cell phones.

Later, the students told their stories, describing classroom floors stained with blood, rooms with upended furniture, and computer screens shattered by bullets. Senior Rebecca Bogart, who survived inside her history classroom, took shelter under her teacher's desk. "I was trying to keep calm and my friend was holding my hand to keep it from shaking," she said. "There was blood all over the floor. You never think something like this is going to happen to you and then it does."[13]

The event horrified the nation and added one more mass shooting to a growing number of gun-related incidents in recent years. However, the aftermath of the shooting at MSD was different from what had happened after these earlier tragedies. The students at MSD took matters into their own hands and began to rally for changes in gun control.

GUN VIOLENCE VS. SCHOOL VIOLENCE

While it may appear that school shootings are becoming increasingly frequent in the United States, they are actually rare. The extensive media coverage given to these events exaggerates school violence. Students are actually more likely to be killed by guns in their homes or in public places than in schools. School shootings tend to draw attention to gun violence, and the media focuses on the moral and cultural issues that might be responsible.

FROM THE HEADLINES

HISTORY OF SCHOOL SHOOTINGS

Although school shootings are rare in relation to other types of gun violence, the United States has a history of deadly school shootings. On August 1, 1966, Charles Whitman, an ex-Marine, positioned himself in a clock tower at the University of Texas, Austin. He was armed with pistols, rifles, and a shotgun. From his high vantage point, Whitman killed 17 people and wounded 30 others.[14] Once police discovered where the shots were coming from, they entered the tower and killed Whitman.

Another school shooting that received widespread media attention occurred at Columbine High School on April 20, 1999, in Littleton, Colorado. Two student shooters—17-year-old Dylan Klebold and 18-year-old Eric Harris—entered the high school and began firing at students and teachers. They wounded more than 20 people and killed 13 others before killing themselves.[15]

One of the worst school shootings in US history occurred on April 16, 2007, at the Virginia Tech campus in Blacksburg, Virginia. Seung-Hui Cho attended school at the university and began shooting people a little after seven o'clock in the morning that day. He was armed with hundreds of rounds of ammunition and

In 2018, empty shoes were placed outside the US Capitol. They represented children who died from gun violence.

two guns. Thirty-two people died from his attack.[16] Cho killed himself as police closed in on him.

Another shooting that shocked the nation occurred on December 14, 2012, at Sandy Hook Elementary School in Newtown, Connecticut. Twenty-year-old Adam Lanza entered the school and killed 6 adults and 20 students.[17] Lanza also killed himself before police could take him into custody.

CHAPTER TWO

WHO WAS
THE SHOOTER?

After an act of violence, people usually want to know about the person who perpetrated it. It is common to hear neighbors and friends of the perpetrator say that the person was quiet and didn't seem like the type to commit a violent act. Some people add that there was no warning of the danger brewing beneath the surface. But in the case of the MSD High School shooting, there were clear warning signs that Cruz had the potential to carry out a deadly attack.

AN ADOPTED SON

Lynda and Roger Cruz of Parkland, Florida, had married late in life. It was Roger's second marriage, and he already had children. But Roger and Lynda wanted

Many school shooters end up either committing suicide or being killed by police. However, police were able to find and arrest Nikolas Cruz.

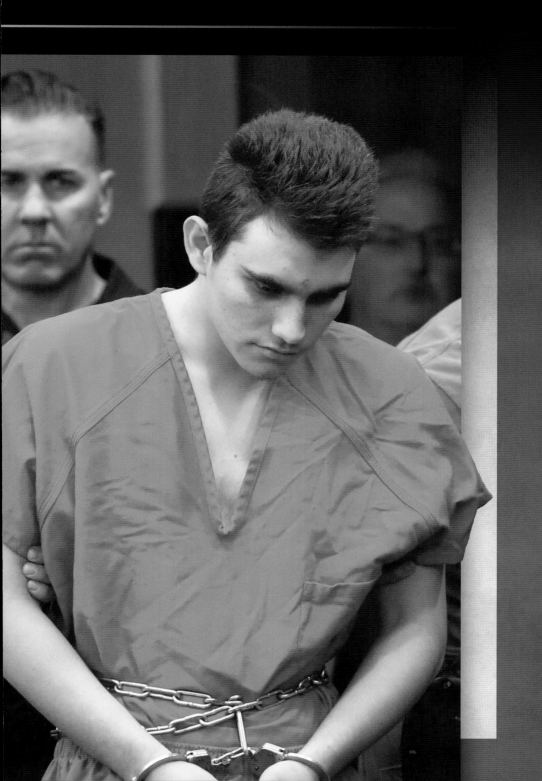

children of their own, and they arranged for a private adoption through an attorney. The attorney located a mother who passed a series of drug tests and was willing to give up her baby for adoption. The baby's father was unknown. On September 24, 1998, Lynda was in the delivery room when Cruz was born. The nurse wrapped him in a blanket and handed him to her.

A year after Cruz was born, his parents adopted another son from the same mother and named him Zachary. Cruz appeared to have a good life with his adoptive parents. The family lived in a house they'd built in Parkland. It had a pool and a big backyard. The boys had a good relationship with their father, who was a businessperson and spent a lot of time with his kids. Lynda was a stay-at-home mom who drove her sons to sports practices and helped plan the construction of a new park in their neighborhood. Families

KILLING ANIMALS

One warning sign that Cruz was potentially disturbed and dangerous had to do with his claim that he liked to kill animals. A student recalled Cruz saying that he liked to kill little animals such as frogs and that he shot rats with a BB gun. One classmate, Tyra Hemans, recalled Cruz bringing a small dead bird to class. "I looked close and I saw he was holding a dead bird. . . . That was disturbing." Hemans had known Cruz for several years and remembered him as a loner. "He always stared at everyone. He would stare into your soul."[1]

could buy fence slats in the park's perimeter fence as a fund-raising tool for the park's construction. Those slats were carved with the names of their children. Both Cruz and his brother have their names on slats at Liberty Park. The family was Catholic, and the boys had Communions and confirmations in their church. They seemed to be a happy, normal American family.

But there were signs early in Cruz's life that he had some difficulties. At the age of three, he was diagnosed with developmental delays. This happens when a child does not reach developmental milestones such as talking, crawling or walking, using fine motor skills, or socializing at the usual times compared with most other children the same age. A child with developmental delays may outgrow them and develop at a slower pace, but if the delays continue the child usually has therapy or is enrolled in special educational programs. Cruz's problems were made worse when his father unexpectedly died of a heart attack. Cruz was only five years old, and he was in the room with his father when he suddenly died. Cruz came out of the room crying, and when his mother asked him what was wrong, he replied, "Daddy's dead."[2]

According to records kept by the Florida Department of Children and Families, Cruz was later diagnosed with various disorders, including depression, attention deficit hyperactivity disorder, autism, and an emotional behavioral disability. Once he entered school, Cruz met with counselors and took medications. His mother also took him to private counselors. She said that he also had anger issues and obsessive-compulsive disorder. Neighbors later said that Cruz was devoted to his mother and that she was his best friend and did everything for him.

SON AND BROTHER

Cruz had troubles at home, especially when it came to his younger brother, Zachary. After the shooting took place, Zachary told sheriff's deputies that he wished he'd been nicer to his brother, and he admitted to ganging up with his friends to bully Cruz. Cruz was small for his age, which made him a target for bullies. The sheriff's deputy who spoke with Zachary also said there may have been resentment on Zachary's part because he saw Cruz as being the favorite son. Zachary also mentioned that when he went to play with his friends, his mother would always make him take Cruz along as well, because his older brother had trouble making friends.

Cruz had other difficulties at home in terms of his anger management issues. His mother often called the police because Cruz was physically abusive. Cruz would hit his mother with objects, and he threw her against a

Zachary Cruz attended a hearing for his brother after the shooting.

wall when she took his gaming system away. He punched a wall when she did it again a year later. In ten years, the Broward County Sheriff's Office responded to more than 23 calls from the Cruz household.[4]

SCHOOL DAYS

Cruz didn't have an easy time at school. He developed a reputation for being disobedient and disruptive, using foul language, and insulting students and teachers. At the age of 15, Cruz had to leave Westglades Middle School in Parkland because of his behavior. He was then enrolled at Cross Creek School in Pompano Beach, Florida, which had programs for students with emotional and behavioral problems. Cruz did not want to be there, according to a report from the school system in June 2015: "Nikolas' personal goal is to [be] mainstreamed to his home high school. He often perseverates on the idea that his current school is for students that are 'not smart' and that he can now handle being in 'regular' school."[5] Cruz managed to remain until January of his tenth-grade year. He was very concerned about getting good grades. However, a report from Cross Creek said that he was often distracted by "inappropriate conversations by classmates if the discussion is about guns, people being killed, or the armed forces."[6]

Despite the concern over Cruz's preoccupation with these topics, the school district allowed him to enroll at MSD High School in January 2016. But less than a month after he enrolled there, a young neighbor reported to the sheriff's office that Cruz had posted something on Instagram about planning to "shoot up" the school.[7] When police investigated, they found that Cruz had knives and a BB gun in his possession, and they passed this information along to the high school's school resource officer, Peterson.

Cruz passed tenth grade at MSD High School and returned there after summer vacation. He had joined the Junior Reserve Officers' Training Corps (JROTC) program and hoped to join the

ROTC

The Reserve Officers' Training Corps (ROTC) is a US military program that takes place on college campuses and has junior programs in high schools. It prepares young people to become military officers. At the college level, they receive a paid college education and the guarantee of a military career after college. In exchange, ROTC candidates agree to serve in the US military. JROTC is a popular club at MSD High School. Three of the victims were JROTC members, and Cruz had also once been a JROTC cadet. He was wearing the distinctive JROTC maroon polo shirt during the shootings, which helped him blend in when he left the school afterward.

military after high school. But as he started his junior year, Cruz's behavior took a turn for the worse and he was suspended for fighting. Just before he turned 18 in September, a peer counselor told Peterson that Cruz had tried to kill himself by drinking gasoline and said that Cruz wanted to buy a gun. Under Florida law, Cruz could purchase a gun once he turned 18. Cruz was also reported to the Florida child welfare department after cutting his arms while on Snapchat. He had posted the video to the social media app shortly after breaking up with his girlfriend, whom he said was cheating on him. The department investigated but closed the case in November 2016 after deciding that although Cruz had a mental illness, he was being adequately cared for in an outpatient mental health treatment center and was no risk to himself or others.

Educational experts at MSD High School recommended that Cruz return to Cross Creek School. But Cruz had turned 18 and was legally an adult, and he refused to transfer. He also refused to receive any more treatment by mental health services. A few months later, his mother sold the house that Cruz and Zachary had grown up in, and days later Cruz was given a one-day suspension from school for assault. The school also asked the school district to conduct a threat assessment on Cruz, and on February 8, 2017, he was banned from MSD High School. Days later, Cruz purchased the AR-15 rifle that he would use in his deadly shooting the next year.

THREAT ASSESSMENT

A threat assessment is a group process used to evaluate how much of a threat a student or other person poses in a school environment. It was developed in 2002 by the US Secret Service in response to the many incidents of school violence. A threat assessment is usually done following a perceived or actual threat, or because of some other behavior that causes concern. The student's behavior is investigated by trained experts within the school or school district, and an action plan may be created for dealing with the behavior.

CHAPTER THREE

THE
PROBE INTO
EVENTS

T hrough 2017, after Cruz had been banned from MSD High School, he went to several alternative schools for students who were at risk because of mental or emotional issues, but his attendance was poor. Then an event took place that officials believe may have driven Cruz to the point of carrying out the school shooting. His mother died of pneumonia at the age of 68. Afterward, Cruz lived with several neighbors, and there were more incidents of violence and assault. Cruz was also collecting guns and knives. In late 2017, several anonymous calls were

After the shooting, students from across the nation began to demand better gun control.

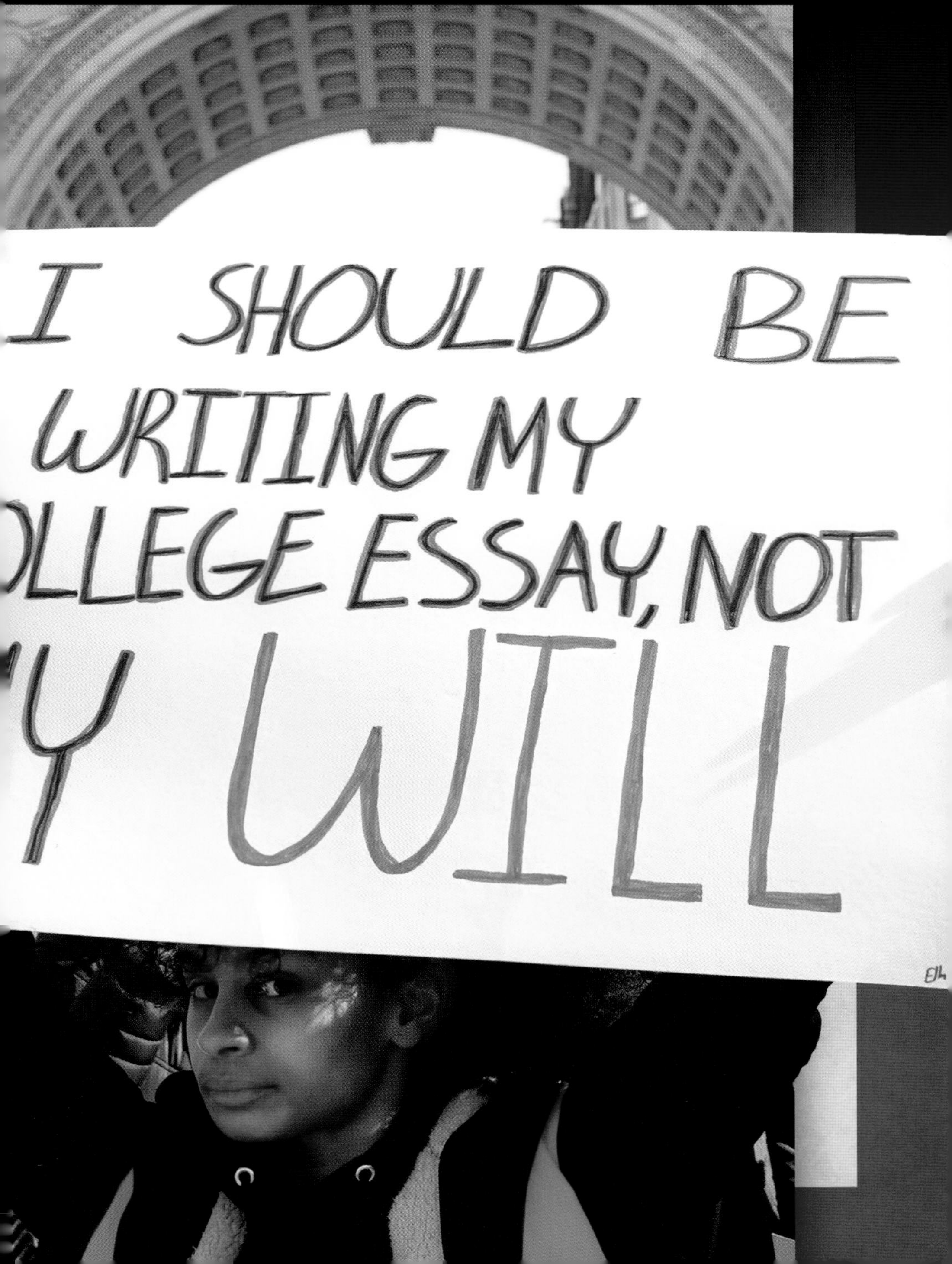
I SHOULD BE
WRITING MY
ESSAY, NOT
WILL

made to the Broward County Sheriff's Office. People told the department that they were concerned about Cruz's behavior. One caller said Cruz "could be a school shooter in the making."[1]

After the shooting, people criticized the Federal Bureau of Investigation (FBI) for failing to take action on many of the clues that pointed to Cruz as a serious threat. In January 2018, the FBI had received an anonymous tip from someone who claimed to be close to Cruz, saying that Cruz owned a gun and had been talking about committing a school shooting. The caller said Cruz had "a desire to kill people, erratic behavior and disturbing social media posts." Another caller had contacted the FBI months earlier, saying that Cruz wrote in online comments that he wanted to become "a professional school shooter."[2] However, the FBI failed to follow up on either tip.

WHY DID THEY WAIT?

As the news of the MSD shooting broke in the national media, people were shocked. Information began to surface about who was on the scene of the shooting, both during the rampage and immediately afterward.

Governor Rick Scott, *right*, spoke to reporters during a news conference after the MSD High School shooting.

School safety deputy Peterson, who was on campus and never entered the school, said that he thought the shots were coming from outside and he took cover behind a concrete column to assess the situation. As the shootings unfolded, students and adults inside the building began calling 911 on cell phones. Dozens of calls came into two different law enforcement agencies: the Broward County Sheriff's Office and the Coral Springs Police Department. But as law enforcement personnel began to arrive on the campus, they had difficulty communicating with each other. Their radios weren't working correctly. This meant that vital information, such as Cruz's location, what he was wearing, and the weapon he was using, could not be shared. According to officials, this may have helped Cruz leave the campus by blending in with other students. It led to extreme confusion about what was going on and where to find the victims, who were scattered around the campus.

Two minutes after Cruz began shooting, Peterson told police dispatchers that he heard what was either firecrackers or shots being fired. He called for patrol cars and asked deputies to block the nearby roads. Although the lack of communication made it difficult to know exactly when other law enforcement officers arrived, there was a record of Peterson telling a deputy three minutes after the shots began that "we don't have any description yet. We just hear shots, appears to be shots fired." As the first deputy on the scene, it was Peterson's responsibility to initially act as a commander. He ordered the deputies, "Do not approach the 12 or 1300 building. Stay at least 500 feet away at this point." It is not clear why Peterson ordered the deputies to stay away from the building. The training given to deputies specifies that they stop the gunman first, then tend to the victims. A deputy is trained to go in and face the shooter alone, if necessary. Peterson did neither. Sheriff Scott Israel of Broward County later explained what he thought Peterson should have done: "Addressed the killer. Killed the killer."[3]

Colonel Jack Dale of the Broward County Sheriff's Office helped analyze the tapes of the communication that afternoon. He noted that because of the communication problems, there was not much accurate information: "First responders have no information as to where the victims are, or where the shooter is or even the number of shooters. So it's difficult in the initial stages for them, from the sounds of gunfire, to determine where the shooter actually is or how many shooters are actually on campus."[4] When the Coral Springs fire department arrived, officials were ordered to wait outside because the shooter

A VOTE OF NO CONFIDENCE

On April 23, 2018, members of the union that represents the Broward County Sheriff's Office deputies held a vote of confidence in Sheriff Israel. This is a vote to find out if the majority of people support a leader. The union president, Jeff Bell, explained the process: "A simple ballot right here, it's a very simple question. I have confidence in Sheriff Israel or I do not have confidence in Sheriff Israel."[5] Issues surrounding the vote included lack of funding for gun equipment and training as well as confusion over department policies and low morale. When the votes were tallied, it was found that 85 percent of the deputies' union members had no confidence in Israel.[6] Some people hoped this vote would urge Governor Rick Scott to remove Israel from office. As of June 2018, Israel remained in his position.

was still active and still in the school. It is the policy of the department that paramedics stay out of an active shooter scene, as it is with most departments nationwide. It was 2:32 p.m., 11 minutes after Cruz had begun shooting, when deputies entered the school and began bringing victims out for medical treatment.

On March 14, 2018, Cruz was arraigned for both murder and premeditated murder for each of his victims. The state attorney for Broward County, Michael J. Satz, indicated that he would seek the death penalty for Cruz when his trial took place. It is rare that the shooter in a mass shooting goes to trial, since shooters are usually killed by police or commit suicide. Of the shooters responsible for the ten deadliest mass shootings in US history, Cruz is the only one to have survived the event.

MSD HEROES

As the victims and survivors left the school and began talking to their friends and families and the media about what had taken place, stories emerged about many heroes—both students and teachers—who helped save others inside the school.

Students left memorabilia for teacher Aaron Feis and student Joaquin "Guac" Oliver at a memorial site.

Three adults died in the shooting. Coach Aaron Feis was the first hero when he went looking for Cruz and shielded several students from Cruz's bullets in a hallway. "He died the same way he lived—he put himself second," a spokesperson for the football program said of Feis. Geography teacher and camp counselor Scott Beigel died as he ushered students into his classroom when the shooting began. His student Kelsey Friend said, "I am alive today because of him." Teacher Melissa Falkowski hid 19 of her students in a closet when Cruz opened fire. "You try to do the best you can for the kids you are supposed to keep safe," she later said.[7] Athletic director Chris Hixon was also killed in the shooting.

Other heroes included Colton Haab, who was 17 and a member of the JROTC at MSD High School. When he heard the gunshots, he got between 60 and 70 people into a room where he saw Kevlar curtains that the JROTC used as a bulletproof backdrop for marksmanship training. The curtains were thick, padded material that couldn't be seen through. Kevlar is the material used in bulletproof vests. "We took those [curtains], and we put them in front of everybody so they weren't seen, because they were [hidden] behind a solid object and the Kevlar would slow the bullet down." Haab added, "I was a little scared. I was more worried about . . . making sure everybody got home safe."[8] Wang, who was 15, was also a JROTC member. He died when he held open a door to allow other students to escape. The US Army awarded Wang a posthumous acceptance to West Point Academy, which is the US Army Military Academy. Martin Duque and Alaina Petty, both 14 years old and JROTC members, were also killed. All three students were awarded the Army's Medal of Heroism for

MSD students and parents attended a vigil for the people killed in the shooting.

their actions at the school that day. The Florida National Guard honored all three at their funerals.

By the close of the day on February 14, the injured had been sent to hospitals and the rest of the students had gone home. Building 12 of MSD High School, where most of the deaths had occurred, was silent and still held the blood and damage from Cruz's attack. But for the students, their families, government officials, and people all over the country who shared in the emotional shock of the day's events, this tragedy was the beginning of a larger movement.

FROM THE HEADLINES

MOVING TO NEW HOMES

After the death of their mother, both Cruz and his brother went to live with a former neighbor, Rocxanne Deschamps, who lived in a mobile home in Lantana, Florida. Just a few weeks later, Deschamps threw Cruz out of her house after he punched walls, threw things, and hit her son in the face. When she called 911, she said, "I'm afraid [if] he comes back, and he has a lot of weapons.

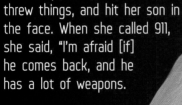

He was just somebody I took in because his mother just passed away. . . . That's all he wants is his gun and that's all he cares about is his gun."[9]

After being kicked out of Deschamps's house, Cruz was taken in by James and Kimberly Snead, whose son was friends with Cruz. While living with them, Cruz followed their family rules, took classes, and got a job. He owned guns, but he kept them locked up, per the Sneads' rules, and had to ask one of them if he wanted to access them. Kimberly later remarked that in the last two weeks before the shooting, Cruz told them that he was happier than he'd ever been before, although he wanted a girlfriend and seemed lonely. On the day of the shooting, he told them he'd be skipping school that day because "it's Valentine's Day, and I don't go to school on Valentine's Day."[10]

Rocxanne Deschamps, *left*, spoke to reporters about living with Cruz.

CHAPTER FOUR

THE
AFTERMATH

O n the day after the shootings at MSD High School, a vigil was held at Parkridge Church in Pompano Beach, Florida. Many MSD students attended, showing their respect for their lost peers and teachers by wearing shirts featuring the MSD school mascot, an eagle. Following the service, 17 balloons were released into the sky—one for each victim.[1] On that same evening, a candlelight vigil took place at an amphitheater at Pine Trails Park in Parkland. The lawn of the park was dotted with large white crosses and Stars of David. Thousands of people attended, some of them students who had witnessed the shooting and lost friends. Parents, teachers, and community members

Students paid tribute to the victims by bringing flowers to the memorial site.

were there, too. Some cried, some prayed, and others comforted each other. The father of a student who died at MSD High School attended, saying, "I don't know what to do next. My wife is at home, and we are broken. What is unfathomable is that [our daughter] took a bullet and is dead."[2]

SEEKING COMFORT

Those who attended the Pine Trails vigil heard from community leaders who tried to bring words of comfort and solidarity. One of the speakers was Anthony Rizzo, a first baseman for the Chicago Cubs baseball team who had attended MSD and graduated in 2007. He told the audience:

> While I don't have all the answers, I know that something has to change, before this is visited on another community, and another community, and another community. We don't know who's hiding their sadness or feelings of guilt and loneliness, or who needs help and is too proud or afraid to ask. So we have to be there for each other, we have to cope with our pain, and we have to live each other's pain.[3]

The vigil ended after a few hours, and most adults left. However, the students remained and sat in small groups on the grass, talking, hugging, and praying. For many of them, it was the first time they had seen their friends and classmates since the shooting. Many of them needed to tell each other their stories of the shooting, discuss what they had seen and experienced, and share their grief. They remained together at the park until sheriff's deputies made the rounds and gently told them that they needed to leave.

THE FUNERALS BEGIN

On Friday, February 16, the first funerals took place for victims of the MSD shooting. One was for Alyssa Alhadeff, who was 14 years old. So many people came that they overflowed from the chapel and atrium. Some people had to stand on the lawn. Her mother, Lori, remembered her daughter and urged her classmates to share stories and memories of their friends. "Honor Alyssa,"

CONSPIRACY THEORY

Hours after the shootings took place, a conspiracy theory circulated through social media and the internet. It claimed that many of the students seen outside the school after the shooting were crisis actors. This is a term used to describe people who act like victims during emergency drills. The implication was that mass shootings were really just staged events to achieve political goals. Student David Hogg, who was outspoken about gun control following the shootings, was the main victim of the conspiracy theories, which claimed he was a crisis actor. MSD students and members of mainstream media have worked hard to debunk these claims about Hogg.

> "I'M PISSED. IT WAS MY DAUGHTER I AM NOT GOING TO SEE AGAIN. SHE IS NOT HERE. SHE IS NOT HERE. SHE IS IN NORTH LAUDERDALE AT WHATEVER IT IS, KING DAVID CEMETERY, THAT IS WHERE I GO TO SEE MY KID NOW."[5]
>
> —ANDREW POLLACK, WHOSE DAUGHTER, MEADOW, DIED IN THE MSD SHOOTING

she said. "Breathe for Alyssa. Do something good with your life." Lori had been interviewed on CNN immediately following the shooting and was remembered for her furious comment as she stared right into the camera and addressed President Donald Trump, saying, "This is not fair to our families, that our children go to school and have to get killed! Do something! Action! We need it now!"[4] She was not the only family member or friend of a victim to call for changes to gun laws in the immediate aftermath of the shootings.

More funerals followed. One funeral was for Carmen Schentrup, an honor student whose letter telling her that she was a National Merit Scholar finalist arrived the day after she died. Visiting hours were also held for two of the teachers who died, Hixon and Feis. More funerals followed each day until every victim had been laid to rest. Most of the services were attended by hundreds of mourners.

TWEETS AND MORE TWEETS

Forms of social media such as Facebook, Twitter, and Instagram have made it possible for people to respond immediately to tragic events. Following the MSD shooting, President Trump issued a condolence through Twitter, saying, "My prayers and condolences to the families of the victims of the terrible Florida shooting. No child, teacher or anyone else should ever feel unsafe in an American school."[6] However, the next day he seemed to place some of the blame on the students themselves when he said, "So many signs that the Florida shooter was mentally disturbed, even expelled from school for bad and erratic behavior. Neighbors and classmates knew he was a big problem. Must always report such instances to authorities, again and again!"[7] This remark angered many people who read it, especially students from MSD High School.

A subsequent tweet by Trump claimed that the FBI had missed clues about Cruz as a potential threat because it was too involved investigating accusations that his presidential campaign had colluded with the Russian government. This further enraged Twitter users. The users accused him of caring about himself and the Russian scandal more than the 17 people who died. Twitter quickly became a platform for MSD High School students to begin the activism that would result from the tragedy.

THE FIRST DAY BACK

On February 28, exactly two weeks after the shootings, students returned to MSD High School. Some students had attended an orientation the previous Sunday to help them get ready for their return and to be with their friends and classmates. It was a difficult day for all students. Many of them felt that it was too soon to return to school or were frightened to revisit the site of the shootings. Others simply wanted to return to their routines. The first day

Therapy dogs at MSD High School were there to help students with the healing process.

was a half day. It was a chance for students to reunite with classmates and teachers or visit the grief counselors and therapy dogs that were on hand to help them. Students would not be expected to return to a full class routine yet. Principal Ty Thompson wrote on Twitter, "There is no need for backpacks. Come ready to start the healing process and #RECLAIM THE NEST."[8]

CANINE COMFORT

One source of comfort following the shootings was therapy comfort dogs. These dogs are specially trained to comfort people after disasters and traumatic events. The dogs were brought to schools around the community, as well as churches and hospitals. They even visited the 17 crosses outside the high school. The dogs, mostly golden retrievers, came from Illinois Lutheran Church Charities (LCC). The dogs let people hug them and pet them. They also sat next to people as quiet companions. "It doesn't take away their pain and suffering, but it does take them to a different place for that special moment," said Richard Martin of the LCC K-9 Comfort Dog Ministry.[9]

While healing was beginning for the student survivors, what happened at MSD High School on February 14 would turn out to be the beginning of something extremely powerful. The students from MSD were angry, and they were not going to return quietly to their routines.

CHAPTER FIVE

NEVER
AGAIN

Mass shootings starting in the late 1990s in the United States have followed a similar pattern: the event saturates the media for days, people express thoughts and prayers in the news and on social media, and soon the news cycle moves on to different stories. However, the shooting that took place at MSD High School did not follow this pattern. The event sparked a huge movement for gun control—largely due to the efforts of the students whose friends and teachers died. These MSD students, in the midst of their grief, were angry and weren't afraid to show it.

Students and adults from Parkland traveled to the Florida capitol building for their #NeverAgain movement.

THOUGHTS AND PRAYERS

Sheryl Acquaroli, 16, from MSD, told Florida legislators, "Thoughts and prayers won't stop my brothers and my sisters from dying—action will. They are our students, our teachers and our coaches. And they died because you failed."[2] She was referencing, in part, what has become a trend: when a horrible event such as a mass shooting occurs, people will send their thoughts and prayers online. Some people believe that with so much repetition of the same response, the words become meaningless. Critics also point out that the response of prayers and thoughts implies that the sender isn't willing to do anything concrete about the problem.

GONZÁLEZ SPEAKS OUT

On February 17, just a few days after the shooting, MSD senior Emma González attended a gun control rally in Fort Lauderdale, Florida. González knew she wanted to stir up the crowd with her message, as she told talk show host Ellen DeGeneres during an interview: "I knew I would get my job done properly at that rally if I got people chanting something. And I thought 'We call B.S.' has four syllables, that's good, I'll use that. I didn't want to say the actual curse words . . . this message doesn't need to be thought of in a negative way at all."[1]

González's speech at the rally started with the admission that every single person on the platform should have been home grieving for their lost classmates, "But instead we are up here standing together because if all our

MORE TO THE
STORY

ABOUT EMMA GONZÁLEZ

In just one week, González went from being a high school senior to a highly visible activist for preventing gun violence. At MSD High School, she had been part of the astronomy club and the Gay-Straight Alliance. She planned to go to the New College of Florida in Sarasota in the fall of 2018. While she was still in high school, her focus was on keeping the momentum of #NeverAgain going. "We are going to be the kids you read about in textbooks," she says. "Not because we're going to be another statistic about mass shooting in America, but because . . . we are going to be the last mass shooting."[3]

However, the MSD shooting was not the last mass shooting. On May 18, a little more than three months after the MSD shooting, a student from Santa Fe High School in Texas opened fire at the school. He killed two teachers and eight students.[4]

government and President can do is send thoughts and prayers, then it's time for victims to be the change that we need to see." González went on to make a powerful speech that has resulted in many people considering her to be a hero and the voice of a new generation, urging listeners to "call BS" on government politicians, the portrayal of teens in the media, the influence of the National Rifle Association (NRA)—a progun organization— on politics, and the idea that tougher gun laws would not reduce gun violence.[5]

THE POWERFUL NRA

The National Rifle Association (NRA) has a lot of power in American politics. But why? It spends a great deal of money supporting political candidates and helping them get elected through campaign contributions and endorsements. In return, those candidates will often vote according to the NRA's position on issues. The NRA also has a membership of millions of people, many of whom are politically active and will support whatever platform the NRA endorses. If a candidate does not act in agreement with the NRA, the candidate has less of a chance of getting elected in certain states where gun ownership is high.

THE MOVEMENT BEGINS

The fledgling activist movement started by MSD students soon after the shooting was named Never Again. The movement was known on Twitter as #NeverAgain and #Enoughisenough. Its purpose was to advocate for stricter background checks for gun purchases. Background checks in part look at someone's criminal history. Some people believe stricter background checks could stop more people with a violent history from purchasing guns. In addition, the #NeverAgain movement planned to stage a nationwide protest on March 24, 2018, called March for Our Lives.

Even as the emotional funerals for students continued, the student organizers knew that this was the time to create their group, while the media and reporters were still in Parkland. They knew that the media's attention span was very short, and if they waited a week, the media would already have left. As 17-year-old Cameron Kasky said in February 2018 to DeGeneres on her show:

The thing that inspired us to create the march was people saying, "You are all talking about gun control, and this is not the time to talk about gun control—this is the time to grieve and time to mourn". . . . And we understand that, and we said, now might not be the time to talk about gun control. Here's the time to talk about gun control: March 24th.[6]

Student survivors, *left to right*, Emma González, David Hogg, Cameron Kasky, and Alex Wind were vocal supporters of gun control after the shooting.

Kasky also wrote an opinion piece for CNN and then went on to do more television interviews. On the evening of the candlelight vigil in Pine Trails Park, Kasky invited some of his friends to his home after the vigil to attempt to start a movement. They wanted to create a central social media space for everyone to come together and spark political change concerning gun violence and gun control. Kasky came up with the name #NeverAgain. Kasky and his friends decided that the movement would be nonpartisan—not affiliated with any political party. They stayed up all night creating social media accounts for the new movement and deciding what needed to be said.

The #NeverAgain movement had various proposals on how to prevent school shootings. Some of the proposals included banning semiautomatic weapons and accessories that can allow shooters to fire more bullets. The students also wanted a database created that can record who purchases guns and what types of guns are bought. In addition, the students proposed that better communication is needed between law enforcement and health-care workers to prevent dangerous people from buying guns. The students also requested that the firearm purchase age be raised from 18 to 21.

GOING TO TALLAHASSEE

At the same time, another MSD student had a different plan. Seventeen-year-old Jaclyn Corin was junior class president, and she had lost her friend Joaquin Oliver in the shooting. Corin posted on Instagram, "PLEASE contact your local and state representatives, as we must have stricter gun laws IMMEDIATELY." Corin spoke with Democratic Florida congresswoman Debbie Wasserman Schultz and to other state representatives. Soon Corin, with help from others, made arrangements to hire a bus to carry 100 MSD students and chaperones to the state legislature at Tallahassee, Florida, the state capital.[8]

The MSD students went to Tallahassee on the evening of February 20 and spent the night at the Tallahassee Civic Center. They were greeted by hundreds of students from Leon High School in Tallahassee, who waved signs of support for the MSD students. Sarah Chadwick, an MSD student, told the crowd, "Our message is very simple— never again." Another student, Sophie Whitney, said, "We're fighting for you guys, we're fighting for the friends we lost, we're fighting for the future kids that we're going to have."[9]

The next morning, the MSD students arrived at the statehouse in three buses. The plan was to meet with legislators and then attend a midday rally. However, despite speaking with government officials about the need for stricter gun laws, the students left feeling disappointed. They felt that the only way they were going to create change

"THE RIGHT TO BEAR ARMS . . . DOES NOT AND NEVER WILL OVERPOWER THE INDIVIDUAL'S RIGHT TO LIFE, LIBERTY AND THE PURSUIT OF HAPPINESS. . . . WE CANNOT PROTECT OUR GUNS BEFORE WE PROTECT OUR CHILDREN."[10]

—FLORENCE YARED, MSD STUDENT, SPEAKING AT THE #NEVERAGAIN RALLY ON FEBRUARY 21, 2018 was by voting, not by meeting elected officials. In an article in the South Florida *Sun-Sentinel* newspaper, 17-year-old student Delaney Tarr expressed the students' frustration by saying, "Coming here today . . . was very disappointing. . . . We've spoken to only a few legislators and try as they might, the most we've gotten out of them is, 'We'll keep you in our thoughts. You're so strong. You're so powerful.' We've heard enough of that. . . . That is not why we're here today. We're not here to be patted on the back."[11]

"AMERICA'S HIGH SCHOOL STUDENTS ARE LEADING A REVOLUTION AGAINST POLITICAL COMPLACENCY AND COLLUSION. . . . AND I WANT YOU TO KNOW THAT YOU ARE NOT ONLY ACTING IN SOLIDARITY WITH THE STUDENTS FROM PARKLAND . . . BUT YOU ARE ACTING IN THE FINEST TRADITION OF AMERICA'S YOUNG PEOPLE WHO HAVE ALWAYS STOOD UP TO CHANGE AMERICA WHEN NOBODY ELSE WOULD DO IT."[12]

—JAMIE RASKIN, US CONGRESSMAN FOR MARYLAND, SPEAKING IN WASHINGTON, DC, ON FEBRUARY 21, 2018

While the MSD students met with legislators, other gun control supporters were rallying on the steps of the Florida capitol. After the meetings, many of those supporters marched into the statehouse. As legislators came out to meet the students, the legislators were greeted with shouts about gun control and passing the stalled bill to

Florida senator Bobby Powell spoke with students from MSD when they visited Tallahassee.

ban assault weapons. At the time, this bill, which included a ban on assault-style weapons as well as new limitations on gun sales, was being hotly debated in the Florida House. Sixteen-year-old Alfonso Calderon of MSD High School expressed the disappointment in the government process that most of the students felt, saying, "I don't know if I'm going to have faith in my state and local government anymore, because what I saw today was

"WE ARE JUST CHILDREN. A LOT OF PEOPLE THINK THAT DISQUALIFIES US FROM EVEN HAVING AN OPINION ON THIS SORT OF MATTER. . . . THIS MATTERS TO ME MORE THAN ANYTHING ELSE IN MY ENTIRE LIFE."[13]

—ALFONSO CALDERON, MSD STUDENT, SPEAKING TO TALLAHASSEE LAWMAKERS ON FEBRUARY 21, 2018 discouraging. This is something serious. It's about human lives."[14]

It was clear to the MSD students that pushing for gun control would take more than just meetings with elected officials. The #NeverAgain movement, thanks to social media, had spread around the world. The movement included global issues such as human and civil rights. It was time to make a bigger statement to try to keep tragedies like MSD's from happening again.

LEGISLATIVE HEARTBREAK

Before the MSD students bused to Tallahassee on February 20, several students were in the state legislature watching when a vote was taken concerning taking up a bill to ban assault rifles and large-capacity magazines. The legislature voted down the bill, 36–71, which meant that the bill would not be brought up during that year's session, effectively killing it.[15] The students watched from the gallery in disbelief, and several broke down in tears.

CHAPTER SIX

MARCH FOR
OUR LIVES

T he student survivors of the shootings at MSD High School were grieving, but they were also angry. They had started the #NeverAgain movement, they had gone to their state government without much success, and they were making themselves heard on social media and in the regular news media about gun control. But many felt something bigger was needed.

NATIONAL SCHOOL WALKOUT

The students called for a National School Walkout day on March 14, 2018. The walkout was planned both as a memorial to the students who died and as a protest action. Specifically, participants demanded

Emma González addressed a crowd during a March for Our Lives event. She stood silently for minutes to remember the victims of the shooting.

that Congress ban assault weapons, require universal background checks for anyone wanting to purchase a weapon, and pass a law allowing courts to take guns away from people who had shown signs of violent behavior.

Students, staff, and teachers all over the United States were urged to walk out of their schools for 17 minutes—one minute for each death at Parkland. The idea for the march originated with the Women's March EMPOWER initiative. The Women's March was a series of organized marches to protest many of President Trump's policies and actions relating to women's issues. EMPOWER distributed school-walkout tool kits to student organizers to help their student groups get started. The kits included a step-by-step organization guide with advice about planning the event, getting adult support, and advertising the walkout, plus a sample letter to administrators requesting permission to participate and an explanation of the rights students have.

Schools at the K–12 level, especially middle and high schools, had mixed reactions to students participating in the walkout. Some allowed it, some suggested alternative ways for students to protest and remember, and some

MORE TO THE
STORY

WHAT ARE
STUDENTS' RIGHTS?

Schools can punish students for missing class to join a walkout, but schools can't punish students any more than they would for any other class-skipping incident. Students are allowed by the First Amendment to protest, and schools that forbid students to protest could face legal repercussions. According to Vera Eidelman, a fellow at the American Civil Liberties Union, a nonprofit group that protects constitutional rights, "What the school can't do is discipline students more harshly because they are walking out to express a political view or because school administrators don't support the views behind the protest."[1]

In 1969, the Supreme Court case *Tinker v. Des Moines Independent Community School District* ruled that students have the right to free speech while in school. The case centered on a group of students who were suspended after wearing black armbands at school. They wore the armbands to protest the Vietnam War (1954–1975).

threatened disciplinary action for any student who did walk out. These actions could include suspensions, unexcused absences, or a bad grade in any class they missed.

Many colleges and universities noted that if aspiring college students were punished by their schools, the students' applications to the college or university would not be affected and their chances for admission would not be jeopardized. Yale University's assistant director of admissions, Hannah Mendlowitz, stated, "Yale will NOT be rescinding anyone's admission decision for participating in peaceful walkouts for this or other causes, regardless of any high school's disciplinary policy. I, for one, will be cheering these students on." In total, more than 117 colleges and universities issued similar statements to prospective students.[2]

Tens of thousands of students in schools across the country participated in the walkouts. Students who lived in the northeast, where a large snowstorm canceled many schools on the planned day of the walkout, either created their own protests outside of school or staged walkouts on the next day when school was open. Some students

Students in Washington, DC, walked out of school and marched on the Capitol building on March 14.

earned detentions and suspensions when their 17-minute walkouts turned into daylong protests near city and state governmental offices.

The Network for Public Education, an organization that works to strengthen public schools, called for another school walkout on April 20, 2018. That date marked the nineteenth anniversary of the 1999 shootings at Columbine High School. The organization urged students and schools to create their own events to bring attention to gun safety. However, unlike the earlier walkout, this one was not as strongly supported by secondary schools. Many students faced suspension for participating.

ORGANIZING THE MARCH

While the National School Walkout was largely created and organized by EMPOWER, the March for Our Lives, which took place on March 24, 2018, was created by MSD students. In an interview with DeGeneres, Kasky spoke about the decision to hold the march after being told that students should take the time to grieve before they began demonstrating: "It's amazing the universal support we've gotten. It's proof that this isn't red and blue, this isn't generation versus generation—this is the 97 percent of people who believe we need to take steps here together."[3]

According to the March for Our Lives website, the focus was to make sure that special interest groups or political agendas would not get in the way of the timely passage of gun control laws and addressing gun violence. Specifically, the march was to work for universal and comprehensive background checks; updating the Bureau of Alcohol, Tobacco, Firearms and Explosives with a digital database of information; funding research about gun violence in the United States; and banning assault weapons and high-capacity ammunition magazines.

March for Our Lives involved huge gatherings of people in cities all over the country, and even globally. But how did a group of high school students from Florida organize such a wide-reaching event? The key was that they began organizing protests for gun control immediately after the shootings, when they wouldn't have been expected to be rallying yet. They knew that media attention was something they had to take advantage of while they had it—especially the opportunity they had of reaching many people through social media. They wanted to not only address gun violence but also protest the involvement of special interest groups such as the

Teenagers created signs for the March for Our Lives event.

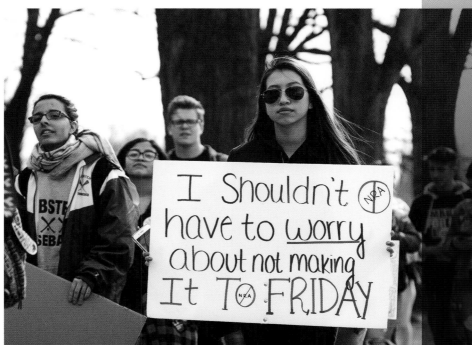

NRA in gun control politics. As González said, "Maybe the adults have gotten used to saying 'it is what it is,' but if us students have learned anything, it's that if you don't study, you will fail. And in this case if you actively do nothing, people continually end up dead, so it's time to start doing something."[4]

March for Our Lives was intended to give students everywhere a chance to "beg for our lives," according to Kasky.[5] The main rally took place in Washington, DC, but events also occurred in cities including Boston, Massachusetts; Miami, Florida; and New York City, New York, as well as overseas in cities such as London, Copenhagen, Madrid, Tokyo, Brisbane, Rome, and Paris.

SUPPORTING THE MARCH

As plans for the rallies developed, people stepped up

to help the student organizers. Fund-raising began with a campaign on the crowdfunding website GoFundMe that raised $1.7 million in just three days. Celebrities, including filmmaker Steven Spielberg, philanthropist Oprah Winfrey, and actor George Clooney, donated $2 million more. These funds paid for the supplies, equipment, and coordination of what would be a massive event. Ultimately, 42,000 people contributed nearly $3.5 million to the online fund-raiser.[7]

Organizations also supported the march. Giffords is a gun-safety advocacy group created by former congresswoman Gabrielle Giffords, who survived a shooting in 2011. The group offered to help some of the MSD families get to Washington, DC. In addition, the New England Patriots football team and its CEO, Robert Kraft, offered some families transportation to Washington, DC,

SANDY HOOK AND THE MARCH

Among the students at the Washington, DC, rally was a group of people who had survived the Sandy Hook shooting. They attended the rally to show their support for the movement. "It felt really good to have so many people supporting the same cause we've been affected by for years," former Sandy Hook student Danielle Agugliaro said. Former Sandy Hook student Mackenzie Casey added, "This wasn't in our power when it happened to us. At this point, almost everyone in the entire country knows someone who has been affected by gun violence, if they haven't been themselves."[8]

on the Patriots' jet. The ice cream company Ben & Jerry's also donated funds for bus transportation to the march.

The group Everytown for Gun Safety, which was founded by New York City mayor Michael Bloomberg in 2014, helped organize and fund marches in Atlanta, Georgia; Chicago, Illinois; Dallas, Texas; Denver, Colorado; Las Vegas, Nevada; and New Orleans, Louisiana. It also gave out grants worth thousands of dollars to hundreds of local organizers nationwide. The money helped organizers get the resources needed, such as money to pay for supplies, equipment, and security for their marches to take place.

Gabrielle Giffords is an advocate for gun control.

A VOICE FOR EVERYONE

The MSD students who organized the rally believed that the media had made a mistake in its coverage of shootings. The media had not paid enough attention to the experiences and perspectives of black communities that had experienced shootings. They were also aware that their school had received more attention in the media because of its location. "We recognize that Parkland received more attention because of its affluence," Corin said in her speech at the Washington, DC, rally. "But we share this stage today and forever with those communities who have always stared down the barrel of a gun."[9]

MSD students invited speakers from areas such as Chicago; Brooklyn, New York; and Los Angeles, California, to participate in the March for Our Lives rally. These speakers came from areas where gun violence was frequent, and they discussed the effects of gun violence on their communities. Yolanda Renee King, whose grandfather was Martin Luther King Jr., joined Corin on the stage following Corin's speech during the rally in Washington, DC. King said she, like her grandfather, had a dream in which "enough is enough." Then she led the crowd in a chant: "Spread the word! Now you heard! All across the nation! We are going to be! A great generation!"[10]

> "THIS MOVEMENT, CREATED BY STUDENTS, LED BY STUDENTS, IS BASED ON EMOTION. IT IS BASED ON PASSION AND IT IS BASED ON PAIN. OUR BIGGEST FLAWS—OUR TENDENCY TO BE A BIT TOO AGGRESSIVE, OUR TENDENCY TO LASH OUT, THINGS THAT YOU EXPECT FROM A NORMAL TEENAGER—THESE ARE OUR STRENGTHS."[11]
>
> **—DELANEY TARR, A SENIOR AT MSD HIGH SCHOOL**

NOT A MOMENT, BUT A MOVEMENT

The March for Our Lives reminded people of the marches that had taken place in the 1960s and 1970s to protest the Vietnam War (1954–1975) and support civil rights. More than 800 groups participated in March for Our Lives events in cities all across the United States, as well as internationally in England, Spain, Japan, and Italy. These countries were also protesting gun violence. MSD student Leslie Chiu pointed out that the march was not just about school shootings—it was about gun violence in general. "This is not just in Parkland," she said. "It is in every community, especially those of color. . . . This is not a moment. This is a movement."[12]

The students vowed that the March for Our Lives was just the beginning. They would continue to work for gun control, but not through more marches and rallies. At the time, midterm elections were drawing close and the student movement turned to politics. However, the students had to contend with strong advocates for the Second Amendment.

FROM THE
HEADLINES

AT THE MARCH

Hundreds of thousands of people attended March for Our Lives events across the country. Many of the marchers wore or carried signs to express how they felt. Some of the most notable signs included "Am I next?," "I'm joining whatever political party those kids in Florida just started," "Your right to rifles. My right to life," "I should be worried about my GPA, not getting shot," "The number of bullet holes in this poster are the number that can be shot in the time it takes to read it," and "The only thing easier to buy in the U.S. than a gun is the president."[13] The last sign was referring to the NRA contributions to Trump's presidential campaign.

At the Washington, DC, rally on March 24, MSD students stepped on stage and demanded better gun control. Musicians such as Lin-Manuel Miranda and Miley Cyrus attended the event to show their support. The March for Our Lives organization estimated that approximately 800,000 people attended the rally, which would make it the largest single-day protest ever held in Washington, DC.[14]

Singers such as Ariana Grande and Jennifer Hudson performed at the Washington, DC, March for Our Lives rally.

CHAPTER SEVEN

THE SECOND AMENDMENT

Almost immediately after the shooting at MSD High School, students took up the cause to fight for better gun control. Although it was an issue of immediacy for them, the shooting also created a tipping point in the ongoing and long-standing debate about whether there should be restrictions on the right of Americans to buy guns.

TO KEEP AND BEAR ARMS

Arguments for and against gun control most often center on the interpretation of the Constitution's Second Amendment. It states, "A well regulated Militia, being necessary to the security of a free State, the right of the people to keep and bear Arms,

People were upset with President Trump and the NRA for not supporting gun control measures.

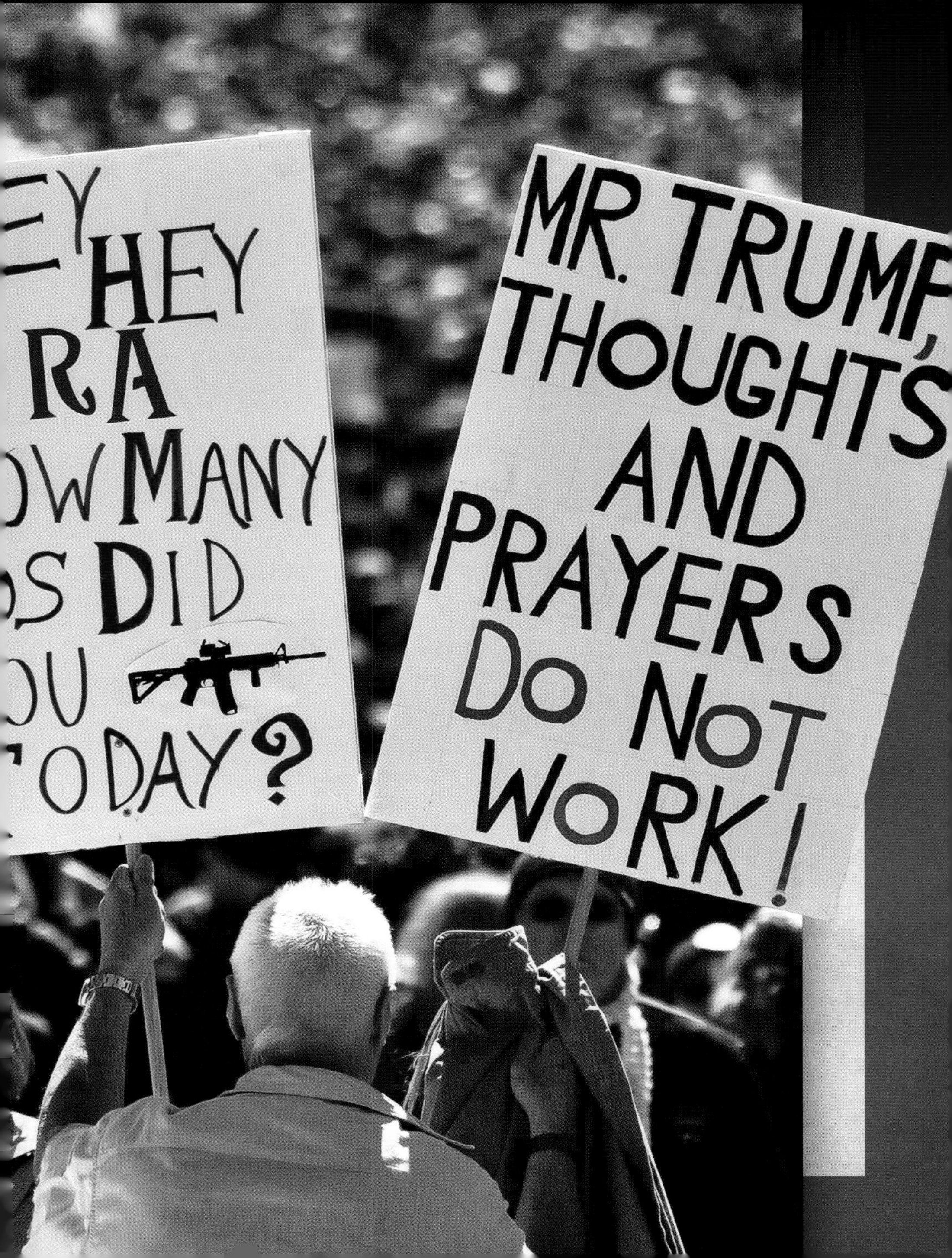
HEY
DID
MR. TRUMP,
THOUGHTS
AND
PRAYERS
DO NOT
WORK!

The Supreme Court has nine justices who listen to dozens of cases each year.

shall not be infringed."[1] Some people argue that this language, particularly "the right of the people to keep and bear Arms," means that every American citizen has a constitutional right to own guns, and that any attempt to regulate this right is unconstitutional. Others say that the amendment was only intended to protect individual states from losing their right to maintain militias for their self-defense. This was especially important because the founders of the United States did not originally support the idea of a standing army, and state militias filled the need for national defense. There are arguments that the Second Amendment is no longer relevant since the United

States now has a permanent military. These people argue that the amendment should be eliminated.

The US Supreme Court has tackled Second Amendment rights in several cases. The first was *United States v. Miller* in 1939, when the court's ruling explained that the Second Amendment was meant to ensure that the military could be effective, not to guarantee individual rights to own firearms. Their ruling stated,

> In the absence of any evidence tending to show that possession or use of a 'shotgun having a barrel of less than eighteen inches in length' at this time has some reasonable relationship to the preservation or efficiency of a well regulated militia, we cannot say that the Second Amendment guarantees the right to keep and bear such an instrument.[2]

The court noted that the right to own a gun was directly related to the ability to use that weapon in a militia, in defense of the country.

However, in the 2008 case *District of Columbia v. Heller,* the plaintiff contested the 1976 Washington, DC, gun ban, implemented by the DC Council, which is the city's equivalent of a state legislature. It was one of the strictest handgun bans in the country. In the 2008 case, the court said the Second Amendment was meant to establish the right of an individual to possess firearms, and the justices struck down the DC gun ban because it violated that right. These two rulings, along with a subsequent ruling in 2010, *McDonald v. City of Chicago*, that seemed to strengthen the case for individual gun ownership rights, show the court's interpretation has changed over the years.

The Second Amendment has become a rallying point for those who feel that gun ownership is a constitutional right and that any attempt to limit any kind of firearm infringes on this right. Some also feel that stricter background checks and waiting periods for gun purchases are infringements.

POLITICAL PARTIES AND GUN CONTROL

There are major differences between Republicans and Democrats when it comes to gun control. Both parties agree on preventing people with mental illnesses from buying guns, preventing gun purchases by people on federal no-fly or watch lists, and requiring background checks for private gun sales and sales at gun shows. However, Republicans favor allowing the concealed carry of handguns with a permit in more states, as well as arming teachers and other school officials, while most Democrats do not. More Democrats than Republicans feel that gun violence is a major problem in the United States. And a majority of Republicans say there would be less crime if more Americans owned guns, whereas one-half of all Democrats say there would be more crime if more Americans had guns.

THE NRA

Central to much of the gun control debate, and very much in the spotlight in the aftermath of the MSD shooting, was the NRA. The NRA was founded in 1871 to advocate for rifle shooting. It developed programs to improve marksmanship and held annual shooting contests. Later it added hunter education, as well as a focus on self-defense and the recreational use of firearms. It also educated police and firearms safety trainers. In 1990, it established the NRA Foundation to ensure funding for firearms-related activities. Today, the NRA has become the most visible organization fighting for gun rights.

The NRA is also one of the most powerful lobbies for gun rights in the United States. It has spent millions of dollars lobbying the federal government to fight against issues that affect gun ownership and Second Amendment rights, including government-funded research into gun violence and bans on assault weapons. According to the Center for Responsive Politics, a nonprofit research organization that tracks lobbying, the NRA spent almost $23 million in campaign donations between 1989 and

2016, and another $54 million on outside spending such as advertisements and lobbying. In 2017 alone, the NRA spent $5 million on lobbying.[3] The organization has the ability to far outspend gun control lobbies.

FOLLOW THE MONEY

In the days following the MSD shooting, students began asking hard questions of Marco Rubio, a US senator from Florida. Rubio had accepted campaign contributions from the NRA, as had other Florida politicians.

In a town hall meeting held by CNN on February 22, 2018, Kasky asked Rubio if he would stop taking money from the NRA. Rubio replied, "The influence of these groups comes not from money. The influence comes from the millions of people that agree with the agenda, the millions of Americans that support the NRA."[4] Rubio did say that he was in favor of raising the age limit for purchasing rifles from 18 to 21, and he was open to considering a ban on certain ammunition magazines that allow a shooter to shoot more rounds more quickly—both of which the NRA opposes.

MORE TO THE
STORY

THE NRA'S MOST
INFLUENTIAL LOBBYIST?

Marion Hammer spent 40 years as the United States' most influential progun lobbyist. A lobbyist is a professional advocate who represents a certain organization or group and tries to persuade lawmakers to vote in accordance with legislation that matches the group's interests. Hammer is the NRA's Florida lobbyist, and Florida has had some of the most lenient gun control laws in the country. She was responsible for developing a state statute that punishes local officials who attempt to establish gun regulations stricter than those imposed at the state level, as well as a concealed carry law that allows Florida residents to carry concealed weapons in public with a permit. She also created the country's first Stand Your Ground self-defense law, authorizing the use of lethal force in response to a perceived threat.

Rubio and other Florida politicians fielded questions and comments from students, parents, and other people in the audience at the town hall meeting. MSD senior Ryan Deitsch asked, "We would like to know why do we have to be the ones to do this? Why do we have to speak out to the (state) Capitol? Why do we have to march on Washington, just to save innocent lives?"[5]

González confronted NRA spokeswoman Dana Loesch and asked her about the NRA's position on bump stocks— which are gun attachments that allow a person to shoot semiautomatic weapons more quickly—as well as making it more difficult for people to purchase certain types of weapons. Loesch replied that the NRA felt that the process for buying firearms is flawed and that the group was awaiting a ruling from the Justice Department concerning bump stocks. González went on to tell

BUMP STOCKS

A bump stock is a piece of metal or plastic that replaces the butt of a semiautomatic weapon, making it fire more like an automatic weapon. Instead of firing one round for one squeeze of the trigger, a bump stock lets the shooter fire hundreds of rounds per minute by holding his or her finger on the trigger and letting the rifle's recoil move it back and forth against the shooter's shoulder. This allows the rifle to fire rapidly again and again. Bump stocks are legal, but Trump asked the Justice Department on March 10, 2018, to clarify its rules about bump stocks in preparation for a complete ban on them.

Loesch that the students of MSD "will support your two children in a way that you will not." González also asked about the NRA's position on stricter gun-purchase laws and outlawing bump stocks. Loesch replied, speaking about Cruz, "I don't believe this insane monster should have ever been able to obtain a firearm." She also added that the NRA doesn't support "people who are crazy, who are a danger to themselves, who are a danger to others, getting their hands on a firearm."[6]

BACKLASH

As MSD student activism continued, the NRA's lobbying on gun-related issues and its refusal to agree with raising

Trump spoke at an NRA convention on May 4, 2018. In his speech, Trump promised to protect gun rights.

the age limit for purchasing firearms hit a nerve for some companies. As a result, several companies announced that they would no longer sell guns to people under the age of 21. It was a way to show support for the gun control movement as well as to protest against the NRA. This is a change from allowing 18-year-olds to purchase firearms, as they are legally allowed to do. These companies include Dick's Sporting Goods, L. L. Bean, Kroger stores, and Walmart. Edward Stack, CEO of Dick's Sporting Goods, said, "When we saw what happened in Parkland, we were so disturbed and upset. We love these kids and their rallying cry, 'Enough is enough.' It got to us. We're going to take a stand and step up and tell people our view and, hopefully, bring people along into the conversation."[7]

"WE ARE NOT AFRAID OF YOU, WE WILL NOT BE SILENCED BY ANYTHING YOU HAVE TO SAY. WE ARE HERE, OUR VOICES ARE LOUD, AND WE'RE NOT STOPPING UNTIL CHANGE HAPPENS."[8]

—TANZIL PHILIP, A SOPHOMORE AT MSD, IN A SPEECH TO FLORIDA LEGISLATORS ON FEBRUARY 21, 2018

In addition to these companies, many others that had offered discounts to NRA members—such as cheaper rates for flights and auto insurance policies—announced that they would no longer maintain their corporate partnerships with the NRA. These companies included Hertz, a car rental company, the First National Bank of Omaha, Metlife, an insurance company, and Delta and United Airlines. In some cases, the decision to break with the NRA was made in response to feedback from customers. The NRA released a statement saying that the decisions were "a shameful display of political and civic cowardice" and the group would find other brands to replace them.[9]

The shootings at MSD High School brought the issue of gun control versus gun rights into the limelight, although it had been a strong source of contention for many years. But would all the attention bring about any changes to laws and government policies?

CHAPTER EIGHT

A TIME
FOR CHANGE

I n the days following the shootings at MSD High School, the students grieved but were also angry. They used the momentum from the media to do something about the deaths of their classmates and teachers. They rallied and protested, they confronted lawmakers, and they organized a movement that included a nationwide march attended by thousands of people. The students were determined to push for gun control changes.

A LISTENING SESSION

On February 21, 2018, President Trump held a listening session at the White House with MSD students, teachers, and parents. The president, along with Vice

Trump greeted MSD High School students when they came to the White House.

SANDY HOOK PROMISE

One of the groups represented at the listening session with Trump was Sandy Hook Promise, an organization started by Mark Barden, Nicole Hockley, and Tim Makris—three of the parents who lost children in the Sandy Hook Elementary shooting in 2012. The organization's mission is to stop children's deaths from gun violence. It works at the community level by training volunteers to raise awareness and educate people on gun violence. Sandy Hook Promise also develops mental health and wellness programs and advocates for state and federal gun control policies.

President Mike Pence and Secretary of Education Betsy DeVos, asked for suggestions and feedback about what could be done to prevent these types of shootings in the future.

Suggestions included increasing school security, creating stronger background check procedures, paying more attention to the role of mental health in school shootings, and banning semiautomatic rifles. Parents and students at the session, many of whom were survivors of school shootings or had lost children to them, spoke emotionally about the need to really start taking measures to prevent school shootings from continuing to happen. Trump also mentioned the idea of arming teachers. He noted that teachers should receive firearm training to protect students.

Mark Barden, whose seven-year-old son, Daniel, was killed during the 2012 shootings at Sandy Hook

Elementary in Newtown, Connecticut, pushed back. He noted that teachers like his wife "will tell you that school teachers have more than enough responsibility than to have the awesome responsibility of lethal force to take a life."[1] He added that if someone entered a school with the intention of committing a mass shooting, he was most likely considering it a suicide mission and wouldn't care if there were armed people there.

The idea of arming teachers sparked responses across the nation. Governor Jay Inslee of Washington noted, "I have listened to the first-grade teachers that don't want to be pistol-packing first-grade teachers. I've listened to law enforcement who have said they don't want to have to train teachers as law enforcement agencies. I just think this is a circumstance where we need to listen. That educators should educate and they should not be foisted upon [with] this responsibility of packing heat in first-grade classes."[2]

Many teachers protested as well. Randi Weingarten,

"I WILL ALWAYS REMEMBER THE TIME I SPENT TODAY WITH COURAGEOUS STUDENTS, TEACHERS AND FAMILIES. SO MUCH LOVE IN THE MIDST OF SO MUCH PAIN. WE MUST NOT LET THEM DOWN. WE MUST KEEP OUR CHILDREN SAFE!!"[3]

—PRESIDENT TRUMP ON TWITTER, FOLLOWING HIS LISTENING SESSION WITH MSD STUDENTS AND FAMILIES

president of the American Federation of Teachers, said, "I am sickened by those doing the bidding of the gun lobby . . . who want an arms race and to turn schools into militarized fortresses by arming teachers. Anyone who wants guns in schools has no understanding of what goes on inside them—or worse, doesn't care."[4]

Teachers also began using the hashtag #ArmMeWith on social media, inviting each other to complete the phrase, such as "arm me with books, not guns" and "arm me with the resources and funding needed to help students experiencing mental health issues, NOT guns." Educator Brittany Wheaton of Utah, who helped start the campaign, said, "If you're an educator, you know that [more guns] is not a solution to stopping the violence that's happening in our schools. Knowing that, I decided to start the #armmewith movement, where ACTUAL teachers give their solutions to what's happening."[5]

A PACKAGE OF LAWS

On February 26, 2018, the Florida legislature debated a package of gun bills designed to prevent another school shooting. The package included a three-day waiting period on all firearm purchases, with the belief that three days is enough time for officials to perform background checks on potential gun owners and also to allow a cooling-off period for people who might want to purchase a gun during a moment of anger or for retaliation. The package also included raising the age limit for gun sales to 21 and letting law enforcement officers temporarily confiscate weapons from anyone who has been identified as a threat to themselves or to others. Lawmakers also included a measure that would lead to allowing some teachers to carry guns at school to protect themselves and their students in the event of a shooting.

However, missing from the package of bills was one to ban high-powered semiautomatic weapons—something the MSD students had called for. Republicans in the

ARMING TEACHERS

Since the MSD High School shootings there have been many suggestions as to how teachers could be armed in the event of a live shooter incident in their schools. Beyond the suggestion that teachers be armed, some of the other policies that have been implemented include giving teachers buckets filled with river rocks, which some people claim could be thrown at a shooter to deter him. A rural school district in Pennsylvania has outfitted all of its classrooms with these buckets of rocks. A school district near Erie, Pennsylvania, provided teachers with miniature baseball bats, similar to those sold in baseball stadiums as souvenirs, to use against shooters. Many of these actions have been mocked on social media.

Florida House of Representatives are largely strong gun advocates, and they were not willing to include that ban. They believed the ban was unconstitutional and would be ineffective.

MORE CHANGES

In addition to Florida, several other states took measures as a result of the MSD shooting. On February 22, Oregon lawmakers passed a bill that bans anyone convicted of domestic violence or stalking, or who is under a restraining order, from buying or owning a gun or ammunition. Part of the intent of the bill was to address relationships other

Governor Rick Scott signed the Marjory Stoneman Douglas High School Public Safety Act in March 2018. This act focused on making schools safer in Florida and keeping guns away from dangerous people.

than spouses and live-in partners, which most of the state's existing gun control laws focus on.

In Rhode Island, Governor Gina Raimondo signed an executive order that established a red flag policy. This policy aims to help keep guns away from people who present a serious threat to public safety. The policy lets law enforcement agencies and officers use all legal means to remove guns from people who have shown a red flag, or warning sign, such as threatening violence either publicly or online. Several other states have similar laws in place, but Rhode Island was the first state to adopt a policy like this after the MSD shooting.

In Washington State, the governor signed a bill banning both the sale and the use of bump stocks. While Nikolas Cruz did not use a bump stock, these devices were used in a shooting in Las Vegas, Nevada, on October 1, 2017. In this incident, a lone man killed 58 people as he shot from his hotel room above a crowd of concertgoers.[6] Bump stocks enabled him to shoot more rounds more quickly.

Trump mentioned many possible ways to legislate an end to gun violence. One measure that he acted on was the federal ban of bump stocks. On February 20, 2018, he sent a memorandum to Attorney General Jeff Sessions, directing the Department of Justice to ban bump stocks. In turn, the Department of Justice submitted a notice to the Office of Management and Budget (OMB) "to ban the possession, sale or creation of bump stocks."[7] The OMB had to review and approve the directive before the policy could be changed. There was also a proposal for improving the federal background check system. On March 23, 2018, the Justice Department proposed its own regulation on bump stocks, rather than wait for Congress to act through legislation, but as of June 2018 it had not yet enacted the regulation.

Also, on the day of the National School Walkout on March 14, the STOP School Violence Act passed in the US House of Representatives, but as of June 2018 the bill had not yet been debated in the Senate. The act would authorize $50 million a year in grants

NRA PRAISE

The NRA supported the passage of the STOP bill. Chris W. Cox, executive director of the NRA's Institute for Legislative Action, stated, "This important bill will help stop school violence before it happens. Identifying individuals at risk for violence is a critical part of securing our schools. This bill will give communities the tools they need to stop school violence through early intervention."[8]

to fund training and other programs for improving school safety, and another $25 million a year for physical improvements to schools to enhance security, such as stronger locks, metal detectors, and better emergency notification and response systems for alerting law enforcement in the case of an emergency.[9] The program would also pay for assessment teams to train students and staff on how to report threats. These grants would be overseen by the Department of Justice.

AT THE BALLOT BOX

After the MSD shooting, some people viewed the upcoming midterm elections in November 2018 as a way to bring about gun control change. Many seats in the Senate and the House of Representatives were up for grabs. Historically, voters between the ages of 18 and 25 are less likely to vote than older citizens. However,

"I KNEW THAT THIS WAS SOMETHING THAT WAS GOING TO HAPPEN, AND THAT WE WERE GOING TO BE THE PEOPLE WHO WERE GOING TO MAKE THAT CHANGE. WE WERE GOING TO BE THE ONES WHO SAT DOWN AND TALKED ABOUT IT AND MADE SURE THAT WE WERE GOING TO BE THE ONES WHO WERE GOING OUT INTO CONGRESS AND TELLING THEM, THIS IS OUR FIGHT NOW BECAUSE YOU MESSED IT UP SO BADLY THAT YOU LEFT IT TO THE KIDS AND NOW IT'S OUR JOB. YOU CAN'T TRY TO TAKE THAT BACK FROM US."[12]

—EMMA GONZÁLEZ, SPEAKING AT A GUN CONTROL RALLY IN FORT LAUDERDALE ON FEBRUARY 17, 2018

because of the shootings, the #NeverAgain movement, and the March for Our Lives, people believed that young voters would be more motivated to vote than ever before. While some adults tend to think that young voters don't bother to vote because they are too lazy or their lives are too comfortable, students themselves say that young people have not voted because they don't feel that they have a voice. But 18-year-old Alexa Clymer, a senior who helped organize a walkout at her North Carolina school, said, "People my age need to start recognizing that our parents can't keep voting and controlling what goes on in this country, because now it's not just them, we're not children anymore."[11]

The students who survived the MSD High School shooting used their voices to protest for change. People

Cameron Kasky questions Marco Rubio during a town hall meeting after the shooting.

believe that, because of this, young students and voters have found a voice. The MSD students have also brought people of all ages, genders, and races into the fight with them. As 15-year-old Amber Mitchell of North Carolina said, "Every day after every single march, speech, town hall, there's something new to attach the public eye, so they don't forget this story. . . . We don't want people to think that this is the end."[13]

ESSENTIAL
FACTS

MAJOR EVENTS

- On February 14, 2018, Nikolas Cruz entered Marjory Stoneman Douglas (MSD) High School in Parkland, Florida. He pulled out a gun and killed students and teachers.

- After the shooting, students from MSD High School launched the #NeverAgain movement. The movement calls for stricter gun control laws.

- On February 20, 2018, MSD students traveled to Tallahassee, Florida, to speak to government officials on gun control.

- A National School Walkout day took place on March 14, 2018. Students across the country walked out of their schools for 17 minutes to protest for gun control.

- On March 24, 2018, the March for Our Lives rally took place in cities across the United States. The march aimed to address gun violence in the United States.

KEY PLAYERS

- Nikolas Cruz had a history of violent behavior and killed 17 people on February 14, 2018.

- Emma González was a student during the MSD High School shooting and became a strong advocate for gun control.

- Jaclyn Corin, a student at MSD High School during the shooting, encouraged people to contact government officials and push for changes in gun control following the shooting.

IMPACT ON SOCIETY

After most mass shooting cases, the media will focus its coverage on the event and the grief that follows. However, soon a new story will pull the media's attention away from the shooting. Students made sure this wasn't the case with the Florida school shooting. They created movements and organized rallies to push for new gun control laws in the United States. Their actions helped bring national attention to gun control.

QUOTE

"We're fighting for you guys, we're fighting for the friends we lost, we're fighting for the future kids that we're going to have."

—Sophie Whitney, MSD student

GLOSSARY

AMPHITHEATER

A round or oval area without a roof, surrounded by seats, and used for outdoor events.

ARRAIGN

To bring someone before a court to answer a criminal charge.

AUTISM

A developmental disorder characterized by the difficulty a person has in communicating with others or in forming normal relationships.

GENERATION

Individuals born and living at approximately the same time.

LEGISLATURE

A body of people who have the power to make laws.

LOBBY

To try to influence public officials.

PERPETRATOR

Someone who is responsible for an act.

PLAINTIFF

The one accusing a defendant in a court of law.

SLAT

A thin, narrow piece of plastic, metal, or wood that is often found in a fence.

SUBSEQUENT

Following after something in time.

SURVEILLANCE

Close observation or watch kept over something or someone.

VIGIL

A gathering where people keep watch or pray at a time when they are usually sleeping.

ADDITIONAL
RESOURCES

SELECTED BIBLIOGRAPHY

Burch, Audra D. S., and Patricia Mazzei. "Death Toll Is at 17 and Could Rise in Shooting." *New York Times*. New York Times Company, 14 Feb. 2018. Web. 12 Apr. 2018.

Feller, Madison. "Emma Gonzalez Shares the Story behind Her Moving 'We Call B.S.' Gun Reform Speech." *Elle*. Hearst Communications, 23 Feb. 2018. Web. 12 Apr. 2018.

Fleshler, David, and Yiran Zhu. "Timeline: How the Stoneman Douglas High School Shooting Unfolded." *Sun-Sentinel*. Sun-Sentinel, 9 Mar. 2018. Web. 12 Apr. 2018.

FURTHER READINGS

Harris, Duchess. *The Right to Bear Arms*. Minneapolis: Abdo, 2018. Print.

Owings, Lisa. *Newtown School Shooting*. Minneapolis: Abdo, 2014. Print.

ONLINE RESOURCES

To learn more about the Florida school shooting, visit **abdobooklinks.com**. These links are routinely monitored and updated to provide the most current information available.

MORE INFORMATION

For more information on this subject, contact or visit the following organizations:

March for Our Lives
marchforourlives.com
The official website for the March for Our Lives campaign includes information about continuing activism for gun control.

Sandy Hook Promise
P.O. Box 3489
Newtown, CT 06470
203-304-9780
sandyhookpromise.org
Sandy Hook Promise was founded following the Sandy Hook Elementary shootings in 2012. Its mission is to prevent gun-related deaths due to crime, accidental shootings, and suicide.

SOURCE NOTES

CHAPTER 1. FEBRUARY 14, 2018

1. David Flesher and Yiran Zhu. "Timeline: How the Stoneman Douglas High School Shooting Unfolded." *Sun-Sentinel.* Sun-Sentinel, 23 Feb. 2018. Web. 6 June 2018.

2. Flesher and Zhu, "Timeline: How the Stoneman Douglas High School Shooting Unfolded."

3. Greg Myre. "A Brief History of the AR-15." *NPR.* NPR, 28 Feb. 2018. Web. 6 June 2018.

4. Flesher and Zhu, "Timeline: How the Stoneman Douglas High School Shooting Unfolded."

5. Robinson Meyer. "The Righteous Anger of the Parkland Shooting's Teen Survivors." *Atlantic.* Atlantic Monthly Group, 17 Feb. 2018. Web. 6 June 2018.

6. Flesher and Zhu, "Timeline: How the Stoneman Douglas High School Shooting Unfolded."

7. Audra D.S. Burch and Patricia Mazzei. "Death Toll Is at 17 and Could Rise in Florida School Shooting." *New York Times.* New York Times Company, 14 Feb. 2018. Web. 6 June 2018.

8. Julie Turkewitz, Patricia Mazzei, and Audra D.S. Burch. "Suspect Confessed to Police That He Began Shooting Students 'in the Hallways.'" *New York Times.* New York Times Company, 15 Feb. 2018. Web. 6 June 2018.

9. Bob Fredericks. "17 Killed in Florida High School Shooting, One of Deadliest in History." *New York Post.* NYP Holdings, 14 Feb. 2018. Web. 6 June 2018.

10. Christine Hauser. "What to Do When There's an Active Shooter." *New York Times.* New York Times Company, 16 Feb. 2018. Web. 6 June 2018.

11. Turkewitz, Mazzei, and Burch, "Suspect Confessed to Police That He Began Shooting Students 'in the Hallways.'"

12. Meyer, "The Righteous Anger of the Parkland Shooting's Teen Survivors."

13. Burch and Mazzei, "Death Toll Is at 17 and Could Rise in Florida School Shooting."

14. "Beginning of an Era: The 1966 University of Texas Clock Tower Shooting." *NBC News.* NBC Universal, 31 July 2016. Web. 6 June 2018.

15. Elizabeth Elizalde. "These Are the Deadliest School Shootings in U.S. History." *Daily News.* New York Daily News, 14 Feb. 2018. Web. 6 June 2018.

16. Sabrina Tavernise. "Motive a Mystery in Killing and Suicide at Virginia Tech." *New York Times.* New York Times Company, 9 Dec. 2011. Web. 6 June 2018.

17. "Sandy Hook Shooting: What Happened?" *CNN.* Cable News Network, n.d. Web. 6 June 2018.

CHAPTER 2. WHO WAS THE SHOOTER?

1. Brittany Wallman, et al. "School Shooter Nikolas Cruz: A Lost and Lonely Killer." *Sun-Sentinel.* Sun-Sentinel, 24 Feb. 2018. Web. 6 June 2018.

2. Wallman, et al., "School Shooter Nikolas Cruz: A Lost and Lonely Killer."

3. Matthew Haag and Serge F. Kovaleski. "Nikolas Cruz, Florida Shooting Suspect, Described as a 'Troubled Kid.'" *New York Times*. New York Times Company, 14 Feb. 2018. Web. 6 June 2018.

4. Wallman, et al., "School Shooter Nikolas Cruz: A Lost and Lonely Killer."

5. Wallman, et al., "School Shooter Nikolas Cruz: A Lost and Lonely Killer."

6. Megan O'Matz and Scott Travis. "Nikolas Cruz's Journey: A Timeline of a Troubled Youth through the Schools." *Sun-Sentinel*. Sun-Sentinel, 27 Feb. 2018. Web. 6 June 2018.

7. O'Matz and Travis, "Nikolas Cruz's Journey: A Timeline of a Troubled Youth through the Schools."

8. Haag and Kovaleski, "Nikolas Cruz, Florida Shooting Suspect, Described as a 'Troubled Kid.'"

CHAPTER 3. THE PROBE INTO EVENTS

1. Brett Murphy and Maria Perez. "Florida School Shooting: Sheriff Got 18 Calls about Nikolas Cruz's Violence, Threats, Guns." *USA Today*. USA Today, 23 Feb. 2018. Web. 6 June 2018.

2. Katie Benner, et al., "F.B.I. Was Warned of Florida Suspect's Desire to Kill but Did Not Act." *New York Times*. New York Times Company, 16 Feb. 2018. Web. 6 June 2018.

3. Linda Trischitta. "Confusion at the Parkland School Shooting—Minute by Minute." *Sun-Sentinel*. Sun-Sentinel, 8 Mar. 2018. Web. 6 June 2018.

4. Trischitta, "Confusion at the Parkland School Shooting—Minute by Minute."

5. Ted Scouten. "Deputies Hold No-Confidence Vote in Sheriff Scott Israel." *CBS Miami*. CBS Broadcasting, 23 Apr. 2018. Web. 6 June 2018.

6. Tonya Alanez. "Deputy Union Says It Has 'No Confidence' in Broward Sheriff Scott Israel." *Sun-Sentinel*. Sun-Sentinel, 26 Apr. 2018. Web. 6 June 2018.

7. Nicole Chavez. "These Are the Heroes of the Florida School Shooting." *CNN*. Cable News Network, 17 Feb. 2018. Web. 6 June 2018.

8. Eric Levenson. "Junior ROTC Student Helped Shield Dozens with Kevlar Sheets in Shooting." *CNN*. Cable News Network, 16 Feb. 2018. Web. 6 June 2018.

9. Brittany Wallman, et al. "School Shooter Nikolas Cruz: A Lost and Lonely Killer." *Sun-Sentinel*. Sun-Sentinel, 24 Feb. 2018. Web. 6 June 2018.

10. Wallman, et al., "School Shooter Nikolas Cruz: A Lost and Lonely Killer."

CHAPTER 4. THE AFTERMATH

1. Julia Jacobo. "Sheriff Promises Florida Vigil Attendees: Politicians 'Will Not Get Re-Elected' If Gun Laws Don't Change." *ABC News*. ABC News Internet Ventures, 16 Feb. 2018. Web. 6 June 2018.

2. Lucas Daprile, et al. "Florida School Shooting: Thousands Attend Vigil at Pine Trails Park Amphitheater." *TC Palm*. tcpalm.com, 15 Feb. 2018. Web. 6 June 2018.

3. Jacobo, "Sheriff Promises Florida Vigil Attendees: Politicians 'Will Not Get Re-Elected' If Gun Laws Don't Change."

4. Emily Witt. "Calling B.S. in Parkland, Florida." *New Yorker*. Condé Nast, 17 Feb. 2018. Web. 6 June 2018.

5. Dan Merica and Betsy Klein. "Trump Suggests Arming Teachers as a Solution to Increase School Safety." *CNN*. Cable News Network, 22 Feb. 2018. Web. 6 June 2018.

6. Alex Leary. "Trump Sends 'Prayers and Condolences' to Victims of Florida School Shooting, Offers Assistance." *Tampa Bay Times*. Tampa Bay Times, 14 Feb. 2018. Web. 6 June 2018.

7. Alana Horowitz Satlin. "Trump Suggests Florida Students Could Have Done More to Prevent Deadly Shooting." *Huffpost*. Oath, 16 Feb. 2018. Web. 6 June 2018.

8. Jack Healy. "Scared But Resilient, Stoneman Douglas Students Return to Class." *New York Times*. New York Times Company, 28 Feb. 2018. Web. 6 June 2018.

9. Erika Glover and Brandon Lopez. "Therapy Dogs Help Those Mourning After Parkland Shooting." *NBC Miami*. NBC Universal, 22 Feb. 2018. Web. 6 June 2018.

CHAPTER 5. NEVER AGAIN

1. Madison Feller. "Emma Gonzalez Shares the Story Behind Her Moving 'We Call B.S.' Gun Reform Speech." *Elle*. Hearst Communications, 23 Feb. 2018. Web. 6 June 2018.

2. Michael Scherer. "Florida High School Students Demand Change to Gun Laws and Boisterous Rally." *Washington Post*. Washington Post, 21 Feb. 2018. Web. 6 June 2018.

3. Diana Pearl. "Everything to Know about Emma Gonzalez, the Florida School Shooting Survivor Fighting to End Gun Violence." *People*. Time, 23 Feb. 2018. Web. 6 June 2018.

SOURCE NOTES
CONTINUED

4. Laurel Wamsley. "'It's Going to be Tough:' Santa Fe Students Return to School after Shooting." *NPR*. NPR, 28 May 2018. Web. 6 June 2018.

5. "Florida Student Emma Gonzalez to Lawmakers and Gun Advocates: 'We Call BS.'" *CNN*. Cable News Network, 17 Feb. 2018. Web. 6 June 2018.

6. Feller, "Emma Gonzalez Shares the Story Behind Her Moving 'We Call B.S.' Gun Reform Speech."

7. Robinson Meyer. "The Righteous Anger of the Parkland Shooting's Teen Survivors." *Atlantic*. Atlantic Monthly Group, 17 Feb. 2018. Web. 6 June 2018.

8. Emily Witt. "How the Survivors of Parkland Began the Never Again Movement." *New Yorker*. Condé Nast, 19 Feb. 2018. Web. 6 June 2018.

9. Ryan Dailey. "Second Wave of Stoneman Douglas Students Arrive in Tallahassee to Waiting Crowds." *Tallahassee Democrat*. tallahassee.com, 20 Feb. 2018. Web. 6 June 2018.

10. AJ Willingham. "Some of the Most Powerful Quotes from the #NeverAgain Rallies." *CNN*. Cable News Network, 21 Feb. 2018. Web. 6 June 2018.

11. Dan Sweeney. "Stoneman Douglas Students Demand Change as Thousands Rally at Capitol." *Sun-Sentinel*. Sun-Sentinel, 21 Feb. 2018. Web. 6 June 2018.

12. Willingham, "Some of the Most Powerful Quotes from the #NeverAgain Rallies."

13. Sarah Todd. "The Astonishing Power of Stoneman Douglas Students, in Their Own Words." *Quartz*. Quartz, 21 Feb. 2018. Web. 6 June 2018.

14. Sweeney, "Stoneman Douglas Students Demand Change as Thousands Rally at Capitol."

15. "With Stoneman Douglas Students Watching, Florida House Declines to Take up Assault Weapons Ban." *Sun-Sentinel*. Sun-Sentinel, 20 Feb. 2018. Web. 6 June 2018.

CHAPTER 6. MARCH FOR OUR LIVES

1. Dakin Andone. "What You Need to Know about the National School Walkout." *CNN*. Cable News Network, 12 Mar. 2018. Web. 21 June 2018.

2. Jackson Richman. "College Admissions: Suspension for 'Walkout' Gun Protests Won't Hurt Admissions Chances." *Washington Examiner*. Washington Examiner, 27 Feb. 2018. Web. 6 June 2018.

3. Madison Feller. "Emma Gonzalez Shares the Story Behind Her Moving 'We Call B.S.' Gun Reform Speech." *Elle*. Hearst Communications, 23 Feb. 2018. Web. 6 June 2018.

4. Emanuella Grinberg and Nadeem Muaddi. "How the Parkland Students Pulled off a Massive National Protest in Only 5 Weeks." *CNN*. Cable News Network, 26 Mar. 2018. Web. 6 June 2018.

5. Michael Kranz. "The Students Who Survived the Florida School Shooting Are Planning Something Big to Take the Fight for Gun Safety Nationwide." *Business Insider*. Insider, 18 Feb. 2018. Web. 6 June 2018.

6. Tom Gerkin. "Florida Shooting: Gun Control Debated under #WhatIf Hashtag." *BBC*. BBC, 28 Feb. 2018. Web. 6 June 2018.

7. Grinberg and Muaddi, "How the Parkland Students Pulled off a Massive National Protest in Only 5 Weeks."

8. Amanda Petrusich. "The Fearless, Outraged Young Protesters at the March for Our Lives." *New Yorker*. Condé Nast, 24 Mar. 2018. Web. 6 June 2018.

9. Grinberg and Muaddi, "How the Parkland Students Pulled off a Massive National Protest in Only 5 Weeks."

10. Petrusich, "The Fearless, Outraged Young Protesters at the March for Our Lives."

11. Sarah Todd. "The Astonishing Power of Stoneman Douglas Students, in Their Own Words." *Quartz*. Quartz, 21 Feb. 2018. Web. 6 June 2018.

12. Grinberg and Muaddi, "How the Parkland Students Pulled off a Massive National Protest in Only 5 Weeks."

13. Daniel Politi. "Here Are Some of the Best Signs from the March for Our Lives Demonstrations." *Slate*. Slate Group, 24 Mar. 2018. Web. 6 June 2018.

14. Jessica Durando. "March for Our Lives Could be the Biggest Single-Day Protest in D.C.'s History." *USA Today*. USA Today, 24 Mar. 2018. Web. 6 June 2018.

CHAPTER 7. THE SECOND AMENDMENT

1. "Second Amendment." *Cornell Law School*. Cornell University, n.d. Web. 6 June 2018.

2. "United States v. Miller: Which Side of the Gun Debate Does It Support?" *Constitutional Law Reporter*. Scarinci Hollenbeck, n.d. Web. 6 June 2018.

3. Brennan Weiss and Skye Gould. "5 Charts That Show How Powerful the NRA Is." *Business Insider*. Insider, 20 Feb. 2018. Web. 6 June 2018.

4. Eli Watkins. "Rubio Stands by Accepting NRA Contributions: 'People Buy into My Agenda.'" *CNN*. Cable News Network, 22 Feb. 2018. Web. 6 June 2018.

5. Emanuella Grinberg and Steve Almasy. "Students at Town Hall to Washington, NRA: Guns Are the Problem, Do Something." *CNN*. Cable News Network, 22 Feb. 2018. Web. 6 June 2018.

6. Grinberg and Almasy, "Students at Town Hall to Washington, NRA: Guns Are the Problem, Do Something."

7. Jack Moore. "These Are the Companies Ending Gun Sales to Buyers Under the Age Of 21." *Newsweek*. Newsweek, 2 Mar. 2018. Web. 6 June 2018.

8. Sarah Todd. "The Astonishing Power of Stoneman Douglas Students, in Their Own Words." *Quartz*. Quartz, 21 Feb. 2018. Web. 6 June 2018.

9. Jackie Wattles. "More Than a Dozen Businesses Ran away from the NRA. How It Went Down." *CNN*. Cable News Network, 26 Feb. 2018. Web. 6 June 2018.

CHAPTER 8. A TIME FOR CHANGE

1. Jessica Taylor. "Trump Backs Arming Teachers During Emotional White House Listening Session." *NPR*. NPR, 21 Feb. 2018. Web. 6 June 2018.

2. Scott Horsley. "Renewing Call to Arm Teachers, Trump Tells Governors the NRA Is 'On Our Side.'" *NPR*. NPR, 26 Feb. 2018. Web. 6 June 2018.

3. Dan Merica and Betsy Klein. "Trump Suggests Arming Teachers as a Solution to Increase School Safety." *CNN*. Cable News Network, 22 Feb. 2018. Web. 6 June 2018.

4. Ray Sanchez. "Trump's Suggestion to Arm Teachers Draws Criticism." *CNN*. Cable News Network, 21 Feb. 2018. Web. 6 June 2018.

5. Claire Zillman. "'#ArmMeWith Books, Not Guns:' Teachers Use Hashtag to Reject Trump's Plan to Arm Educators." *Fortune*. Time, 23 Feb. 2018. Web. 6 June 2018.

6. Doug Criss. "The Las Vegas Attack Is the Deadliest Mass Shooting in Modern US History." *CNN*. Cable News Network, 2 Oct. 2017. Web. 6 June 2018.

7. Meghan Keneally. "How Gun Laws Have Changed in 4 States Since the Parkland Shooting." *ABC News*. ABC News Internet Ventures, 22 Mar. 2018. Web. 6 June 2018.

8. Phil Helsel. "House Passes School Safety Bill a Month after Parkland shooting." NBC Universal, 14 Mar. 2018. Web. 6 June 2018.

9. Keneally, "How Gun Laws Have Changed in 4 States Since the Parkland Shooting."

10. Melissa Chan. "Parkland Students Are Taking Their Activism on the Road This Summer with a 20-State Bus Tour." *Time*. Time, 5 June 2018. Web. 6 June 2018.

11. Danielle Chemtob and T. Keung Hui. "Young People Are Marching in the Streets. Will They March to the Polls in November?" *News & Observer*. News & Observer, 29 Mar. 2018. Web. 6 June 2018

12. Victoria Rodriguez. "11 Empowering Quotes from Emma González." *Seventeen*. Hearst Communications, 15 Mar. 2018. Web. 6 June 2018.

13. Chemtob and Hui, "Young People Are Marching in the Streets. Will They March to the Polls in November?"

INDEX

ABOUT THE
AUTHOR

Marcia Amidon Lusted has written 160 books and more than 600 magazine articles for young readers. She is also an editor and a musician and works in the field of sustainable development. Lusted would like to dedicate this book to the students of MSD High School in Parkland, Florida, the students of Sandy Hook Elementary in Newtown, Connecticut, and all other victims of school shootings. May we never forget you.